Merry
Christmas,
Joey

1972

"MR. CUB"

"MR. CUB"

by Ernie Banks and Jim Enright

A Rutledge Book

Follett Publishing Company

Chicago

A Rutledge Book
ISBN: 0-695-80225-9
Copyright © 1971 by Rutledge Books, Inc. and Jim Enright and Ernie Banks
Prepared and produced by Rutledge Books, Inc. for Follett Publishing Company
This book is available at discounts in quantity lots
for industrial or sales-promotional use through
The Benjamin Company, Inc.
485 Madison Avenue
New York, New York 10022
Library of Congress Catalog Card Number 76-149246
Printed in the United States of America
Follett Publishing Company
1010 West Washington Boulevard
Chicago, Illinois 60607

"MR. CUB"

Contents

To my father and mother, Eddie and Essie Banks, my wife, Eloyce, and our children, all my teammates and the Chicago Cubs' faithful and loyal fans.

Foreword

It is a privilege for me to comment officially and personally on the inspirational Ernie Banks, who has made such a great contribution to our national pastime. His records on the field of play are chronicled in the record books for posterity. More importantly, the admiration and respect for his integrity, sportsmanship and sterling character are affectionately rooted in the hearts and minds of those who know him. He is not only a fine baseball player but an inspiration to our youth and a credit to his generation. We are proud of "Mr. Cub" as a great player, as a National Leaguer, as a gentleman and a solid citizen. I am personally proud to call him a friend.

It is a.human idiosyncrasy that great personalities do not come in for their full share of recognition until they are dead or years away from the triumphs of their talent. I am glad to see Ernie recognized in this book while he is still active.

Warren C. Giles
PRESIDENT EMERITUS, NATIONAL LEAGUE

11

About Ernie Banks

So much can and will be said about Ernie's exploits with a glove and bat there's danger of repetition here. So let me introduce another subject.

Ernie Banks is the greatest single public relations man I've ever seen in sports. At a time when baseball can use all the good press, broadcasting and word-of-mouth praise it can get, Banks is the one sure-fire source. Hardly a day goes by without the mail carrying a complaint or two about the missed autograph, the unanswered letter, the refused personal appearance and other beefs from the public—some reasonable, some not.

No one, but no one, makes more appearances than Ernie. When was the last time you saw him brush off a fan? If he's late answering mail it's because he gets more than any other player. But his greatest moments are right there at the ball park. Ernie Banks has instant rapport with little children. Kids are smart. Without even knowing why themselves, they have an instinct that tells them when an adult really likes them and when the fake is on. Ernie has the ability to make little boys and girls certain that the big reason Ernie came to the park that day was to meet them.

Think about it now . . . isn't one of the reasons you like this game today because at least once, years ago, some hero of yours gave you that kind word you'll take to your grave? That's deep-rooted investment in a sport's future. That's public relations. That's Ernie Banks.

Jack Brickhouse
WGN-TV

A Beautiful Man

The Chicago Cubs have been my beat since 1952. Ernie
Banks has been a member of the Cubs since 1953. During that time I've learned just how accurate Dick Young,
of the New York *Daily News,* was when he said, "Ernie
Banks is a beautiful man."

This Texas-born gentleman has a disposition as
warm as a summer sun in Arizona and an outlook as
bright as a brand-new full moon. Does he have an
occasional cigar? Yes. Will he take an occasional drink?
Sure. But will you find him skipping at the last minute
a previously scheduled gratis speaking engagement for a
lucrative appearance? Never. And you'll never find him
talking bitterly or blaming anyone who has done something with which he cannot agree. In the early days you
could set your watch by his promptness. You still can—
allowing time for autograph signing and friendly re-
marks to the fans. I think of Ernie with deep respect,
and it is easy to smile, remembering the times we have
spent together.

The first and only time I acted as traveling secre-

15

tary for a major-league club, the Cubs' road secretary, the late Bob Lewis, asked me to look after Ernie and Gene Baker during a trip to spring training in Mesa, Arizona. This was in the mid-1950s, and it was fashionable either to take a train to camp or to hitchhike.

This particular night we were in the diner when the train reached Tucson. It was a long stop, and Ernie said he was going back to his room to catch a few winks.

Later, in the excitement of getting off in Mesa, I forgot to wake up Ernie, and the train left Mesa with Ernie still catching a few winks.

The next thing I knew, Bob Lewis and the Cubs' civic host in Mesa, Pat Patterson, were running down the tracks trying to catch the train as it neared a switch just outside nearby Tempe.

Lewis finally rescued Ernie. And after safely enrolling him in camp, Lewis called me. "What a fine secretary you are," he shouted. "I give you just one job to do, and you end up almost losing the franchise. Your fine will be the next three trips sleeping in an upper."

In 1959 the All-Star game was played on a Tuesday afternoon in Pittsburgh, and the Cubs weren't scheduled to play again until Thursday night—also in Pittsburgh. This layover provided the opportunity for Ernie and me to spend two nights and almost two days in Ford City, Pennsylvania, visiting Red Mihalik, one of my longtime basketball officiating partners.

Ernie was dressed up and didn't change for the "little fishing" that Mihalik suggested we do. We hadn't been on the lake more than ten minutes when Ernie felt

16

his first bite. You would have thought he was swinging at a belt-high fast ball right down the pipe if you had seen how fast he reeled in that line. Just as the line broke, letting the fish escape, Ernie's prescription sunglasses hit the water and quickly sank to the bottom of the lake.

Ernie stood up, and I was sure he was going to dive in after them. Instead he said to Red, who was rowing, "Drop the anchor. We're going to fish this spot until I catch the biggest fish in this lake wearing my sunglasses."

When darkness finally came, we returned with a box score reading: countless bites, no fish, one broken line, one lost hook and one lost pair of sunglasses.

By the next day all Ford City was buzzing with the news that Ernie Banks was in town. After lunch on Thursday as we packed for the trip back to Pittsburgh, we looked out the window and saw nearly three hundred bicycles parked along the curbs in front of the Mihalik home. Groups of kids had gathered up and down the block, and Red suggested that we leave through the kitchen door to avoid the mob.

"Naw, we can't do that to all those kids," Ernie said.

A few minutes later, he stepped out on the porch. The roar of the happy youngsters must have been audible in Pittsburgh. One by one he shook their hands and autographed everything they offered. Later, as we drove down Main Street, many of the kids rode their bicycles beside the car, saying and waving good-bye.

I've never, before or since, seen a man inspire such intense enthusiasm among so many youths. It was Pittsburgh Pirates' country, but Ernie Banks was king for a day.

Ernie learns by asking questions. Good friends such as basketball coaches Johnny Wooden and Pete Newell and head coach and general manager of the Green Bay Packers, Danny Devine, have often expressed surprise over Ernie's knowledge of their games.

Ernie also has a remarkable knack for remembering faces and names. The boy from Dallas can identify one of Joe Rosenfield's business associates in Des Moines, Iowa, as quickly as one of Joe Carver's cronies in Benton Harbor, Michigan. He is as much at home having a cup of coffee with the boys in the fire station as he is sipping a vodka and tonic with Jimmy Gallagher, Joe Reichler or Bob Shea in Toots Shor's.

Whenever Ernie talks about Wrigley Field he gets more mileage out of the "friendly confines" than Webster himself. He will talk to four sportswriters and the same number of representatives of radio and television, and it's nine to five each will come away with a different angle for a story.

He always has a fresh tale to tell, and his teammates don't call him "Uncle Josh" for nothing—some of them still don't know when he's pulling their legs.

Baseball writers in San Francisco remember Ernie's first visit to the old Seals stadium in 1958. Exchanging small talk with manager Bob Scheffing, one writer asked how tall Ernie was and what he weighed.

Scheffing answered, "Ernie is 6–1, and never varies more than two or three pounds over or under 185."

"Gee, he looks heavier than that," another writer countered.

"Yes he does, but you must remember one thing: Ernie is wound very tightly," the famous "Grump" deadpanned.

One winter afternoon a sportswriter phoned Cliff Jaffe, the Cubs' publicity director, to check out a trade rumor involving Ernie Banks.

"Sir, I don't know where you received your information," Jaffe answered, "but the vice president who makes that deal had better plan to include himself in it. He won't be working for Mr. Wrigley if he is thinking about trading Banks."

Another trade story: An executive went to Phil Wrigley to discuss an offer from a rival club to exchange a package of players for Ernie. Wrigley listened to the man, excused himself and returned with a dictionary. He tossed it on the table saying, "I'd like you to look up the meaning of the word loyalty. After you do that, never come to me again with talk about trading Ernie Banks."

Pete Rose of the Cincinnati Reds once said Ernie's optimistic talk was divided into three different time slots:

"The first time around all Ernie talks about is the Chicago Cubs' winning the pennant and roaring right through the World Series. Nobody else has a chance.

"The second time around he sadly laments injuries and bad luck blighting the Cubs' chances, but they'll still end up the spoiler, helping to decide who is going to win the pennant.

"The third time he's once again bubbling with re-charged confidence, telling how the Cubs are building for the future and will win it all next year including the World Series. I've never known a player with greater loyalty to his team—win or lose."

At the outset of spring training in 1967 the Cubs gave a two-year player-coach contract to Ernie. After the first two-year pact expired, he was given another contract, covering 1969 and 1970. At age forty Banks has just signed for his eighteenth full season with the Cubs.

Umpire Al Barlick described Ernie as a "sweet-heart who never attempts to show up an umpire."

Tom Gorman, another umpire, said, "I'm not going to let Ernie retire until I do. I wouldn't have any-body to talk to when I'm working first if he hung 'em up ahead of me."

Jocko Conlan recalled the day he called Ernie out on a three-and-two pitch and Banks said, "O-o-o-o-oh, Jocko, you missed it."

"All he did was say that," Conlan said, "as he walked away from the plate without ever looking back. He spoke so that only the opposing catcher and I heard him. That's class in a class guy's manner. When a humpty beefs on a call, they can hear him in Kenosha—and nine times out of ten it's an alibi or a cover-up trying to blame the umpire."

When John "Buck" O'Neil collapsed on the dais

●

at the Chicago baseball writers' Diamond Dinner in January 1970, Ernie went straight to his aid. O'Neil had been his manager when he played for the Kansas City Monarchs, and Ernie said later that he was frankly scared stiff. He stayed at Buck's side during the ambulance ride and didn't leave the hospital until the doctors gave him the all-clear signal. Buck and Ernie have kept up a solid and very special friendship over the years. When Ernie wants to talk, he still looks for Buck.

Of my recollections about my association with Ernie Banks, the most memorable involve Will Rogers and Jimmie Dykes.

During a spring-training trip, the Cubs stopped on the way to Chicago to play an exhibition game in Oklahoma City. In the airport lobby I spotted Ernie with his long arms wrapped around a statue. As I stopped next to him, he said, "Here's my champion. Will Rogers. He never met a man he didn't like. Neither have I. What we need in this world now are a lot more Will Rogerses."

Another spring when the baseball writers were readying their annual predictions for the upcoming major-league races, someone asked Jimmie Dykes where he figured the Cubs would finish if Ernie Banks were not in the lineup.

Dykes answered, "In Albuquerque, that's where."

Yes, Dick Young, you are absolutely correct: Ernie Banks is a beautiful man. I feel privileged to relate his story as he told it to me.

J. E.

21

1

"Johnny Carter Sent Me"

My father always said I was the smallest baby he had ever seen. I was delivered by a midwife on January 31, 1931, and weighed five pounds two ounces at birth. Our family, like the others in the neighborhood, had no money for doctors—and I doubt if doctors were available in that section of Dallas anyway.

We were very poor, and my father often worked from dawn to dark seven days a week. I can remember going without lunch and other times when I went to bed hungry. In fact, I never invited friends home for lunch because there just wasn't enough food, and I was never invited to my friends' homes for the same reason.

The first truck I remember seeing was a welfare truck. It came into our neighborhood twice a month to deliver clothing and food to all the needy families. When

I was five years old, my mother found me a pair of new overalls on that truck. I was so excited about having something new that I even wore them to bed. I would run outside whenever Mamma tried to take them off me to be washed. They were new, they were mine, and I was determined to wear them all the time.

We considered ourselves lucky to live near a chain grocery store. Besides our regular allotment of food-stamp books, this meant we could get some of the store's leftovers, like chicken feet, pigs' feet and vegetables the manager and his clerks considered too ripe to sell.

I walked everywhere—eight blocks to the YMCA, about three blocks to the school playground and a block and a half to the grocery store.

None of our parents had money for a YMCA membership, and nobody realized this more than the instructors at the "Y." When we couldn't sneak in, they would come out and invite us to play softball, basketball, volleyball or touch football.

My father worked for the WPA and picked up a lot of odd jobs on the side. One of his frequent laments was that he couldn't spend more daylight time with the family so he could watch it grow. Three of my four sisters and two of my brothers were born before 1940, so he had to keep on building fences and looking for carpentry work.

As the oldest boy in the family, I did most of the chores. It was my duty to see that the kerosene lamps we used in the house were always filled. We had two wood-burning stoves to provide heat, and I carried in most of the wood to fuel them. One was the cookstove in the kitchen. We got our hot water from a big tank on the side of its firebox. I hauled water in from an outside pump in the backyard so that we would always have a good supply for drinking and washing.

Considering the hardships involved, my mother deserves real credit, for she stressed cleanliness to her children. We didn't have too many clothes and most of them were hand-me-downs, but they were always clean. I think she did more washing than cooking.

Most of the kids in the neighborhood raced homemade scooters. The wheels were at opposite ends of a horizontal board attached to a vertical board on the front end. You pushed the scooter with one foot and held on to the vertical board with both hands. As we grew older we would make believe we were racing in the Indianapolis 500 on Memorial Day.

For us, Christmas was just another day without school, but my scooter racing was the result of the first Christmas present I remember. It was a Lindbergh-type cap attached to a pair of goggles you could pull down over your eyes. My mother got the cap from the Salvation Army or an early version of the Goodwill Industries. We never had a Christmas tree and Santa Claus was almost a forgotten man.

We called Christmas our extra Sunday dinner because my mother never missed preparing a big meal for the entire family on Sunday. It was the one day of the week when my father was home to eat with us, and she really put it on: chicken, black-eyed peas, red beans, rice, corn bread and T-cakes—her own special kind of dessert. T-cakes are like cupcakes served with plenty of syrup and jelly. Even when Mom couldn't get us presents, she made sure we had the best meal of the year on Christmas Day.

Sometime later I was given a BB gun and a bicycle. Dad managed to buy the gun for me, and the bicycle was a hand-me-down from a family friend.

Some of the kids used to go rat hunting in city dumps, but we found plenty of those vicious targets right in our own neighborhood. Rats were a community nuisance, and all the homes were plagued with them. When traps failed, my gun, after my marksmanship improved, was the family's best protection.

The bicycle made a big change in my life, especially when my parents gave me enough money to buy two used tires, a headlight and a horn. The first time my mother ever said "no" to me was the night I brought the repaired bike back home and wanted to use the living room as a garage.

"Get it out of here, right now!" Mom ordered. Reluctantly, I found an out-of-sight parking space for it under the outside staircase.

When I was ten years old, I was literally forced to wrestle for my family's Thanksgiving Day dinner. The day before, my mother had bought a chicken for our holiday meal. In those days you didn't buy chickens already killed, plucked, drawn and cut up. This was a live chicken my mother brought home, and while a pot of water boiled on the stove she snapped the chicken's neck in the backyard. The body continued to flop around. Finally, we put the chicken under a tub and went into the house to get the boiling water. When we returned, the chicken was gone. Somebody had stolen it!

Edna, my oldest sister, noticed spots of blood on the ground, so we followed the trail for about a block. It led to a basement apartment where we found a kid standing guard over our chicken. When he wouldn't give up the chicken, we started to wrestle. I finally pinned him and Edna and I picked up our dinner and went home. The bird still had all its feathers, but my pants and shirt were ripped and covered with dirt.

I really couldn't blame the kid who stole the chicken, but I was still determined he wasn't going to get our Thanksgiving dinner. Maybe I would have made it as a wrestler if he had kept on stealing chickens!

On cold winter nights our stoves would sometimes get bright red from top to bottom, and we were always afraid they would set the house on fire. Usually, my father sat close enough to protect us from one stove and my mother protected us from the other while we did our homework.

My parents have always lived in the South. My father, Eddie, was born in Marshall, Texas, and my mother, Essie, in Shreveport, Louisiana. They met and were married in Dallas.

After all the 1970 birthdays, my sisters and brothers ranged in age in this manner: Edna Mae, 41; me, 39; Ben, who died in November of that year, 37; Evelyn, 34; Estekka, 32; Eddie, 30; Frances, 25; Walter Lee, 23;

Glover Leon, 20; Robert Earl, 17, and Donald, 14. Samuel, who would have been 29, was killed in 1962 at the age of 22.

We were never able to find out too much about what really happened to Sam. He was coming home from a dance one night with some other guys, and they were fooling around with a gun. Somehow the gun went off and killed Sam. I had been with Sam a few weeks before this happened, and I had asked him to come to Chicago and get a job. That way we would have been closer together, but Sam wanted to stay in Dallas.

Our neighborhood generally was a good one because all the families were poor and hardworking. On summer evenings most of our parents relaxed on the front porches, but as soon as darkness fell, they called us to come inside. When it got dark, you went home and stayed there for the rest of the night.

In the next few years I had jobs: shining shoes, working in a hotel kitchen, picking cotton and mowing lawns. It seemed like all the black kids in Dallas shined shoes and nobody ended up making very much money.

Despite their hardships, my parents always stressed togetherness within the family. They taught us love and the importance of right thinking. We had to share everything, from clothes to money and food, and we were glad to give whatever we earned to our mother, who determined where it was needed most. This kind of sharing was my first lesson in teamwork.

I liked cotton picking because it meant getting up early and having a store breakfast with my father. We would be up at five, dress and walk to a little café in the neighborhood, where Dad would have coffee and I would have milk and coffee cake or sweet rolls. I didn't get to eat out often, so this was a very special treat, Dad there at the counter with me.

Promptly at six, a truck would pick up all the cotton pickers at a designated spot and standing up in the back of the truck we would ride about thirty miles into the country.

Each picker carried a huge sack over his shoulder, tossing the cotton into it as he worked. The older men could pick with both hands and toss the cotton into the sack in one smooth motion. I used a different method, crawling along the rows on both knees, picking as I moved.

We would work until sundown, and then the truck would carry us back to the city. At the end of each day, the grower paid off at the rate of two dollars per hundredweight. Five or six dollars was pretty good for a day's work. I never made that much, but a lot of the pickers did.

From cotton picking I moved into my first real business venture: a lawn-mowing partnership with Finis Arbuckle. After Finis had completed his morning newspaper route, we would spend the rest of the day mowing lawns. We charged 25 cents. We could only work if the owner supplied the mower, for we didn't have any; we lost a lot of business not owning our own mower. Still, we divided up plenty of quarters at the end of each day.

When I entered Booker T. Washington High School, I developed a new interest—sports. Sometimes it was softball, other times basketball or touch football —whichever sport was in season.

In my first softball game Woody Culton, the recreation director, assigned me to shortstop. I didn't set the world on fire, but Woody kept encouraging me to practice. After one of these games on campus—that's what we called the playground—Culton recommended me to J. W. Worlds, who sponsored the best fast-pitch softball team in our community. Worlds gave me a tryout, and before long I became his regular shortstop.

I might never have played high school football if Culton hadn't spotted me on the sidelines watching while the Booker T. Washington Bulldogs were working out. Culton suggested to coach Raymond Hollie that he give me a tryout.

"Banks can handle himself. I think he may be able to help you," Culton told Hollie.

Later Hollie sent me to the locker room for a uniform. I felt seven feet tall and twice the size of Bronko Nagurski as I pulled on all the padded equipment and a helmet.

After that first drill I told my mother I had reported to the football team. She accepted it with one warning: "Don't get hurt, and don't try to play if you do."

Coach Hollie played me at end. The fellows, especially Carl Williams, our quarterback, always called me the Bulldogs' slow end. Joe Kervie was our fast end.

I've never known a man who coached with more dedication than Coach Hollie. He made us practice until dark, and if you made a mistake, he rapped you across the rump with a board he always carried. My parents didn't get a chance to see me play until the last game of my senior year, and—wouldn't you know—that was the only time I was hurt!

I was introduced to basketball when our English teacher, C. L. Dennard, had each of us write an essay on the game. Everybody flunked. I didn't know a dribble from a rebound. After all, our basketball had been limited to pickup games on outdoor courts; we didn't have a gymnasium.

Dennard followed up the writing assignment with a lecture. It was one of the most interesting I had ever heard, and some twenty new basketball players were born immediately. Later I found out that Dennard was also a high school basketball official.

The summer between my freshman and sophomore years I tried to get a job working with my father. He had left the WPA and hired out as a stock clerk for a grocery chain. I figured there might be an opening for me, but whenever I asked him he would say, "No son, the work is too hard. You aren't old or strong enough yet."

Later I learned his talk was a cover-up. There were frequent fights between the blacks and whites on the job and a lot of name-calling. My dad didn't want me exposed to it. So I did odd jobs and spent most of that summer playing softball for Worlds' team. We traveled to cities in the Dallas area, and the team turned into a big winner.

During one game in Dallas, Hank Thompson—later a star third baseman for the New York Giants—was playing for our opponents. I had heard about Thompson's outstanding hitting ability, and I watched every move he made with a bat. With just one smooth swing, Hank hit a ball onto the roof of a house behind the outfield fence. It was the longest home run I had ever seen in softball.

Other home-run balls had hit that house, but none had hit with the velocity of Thompson's. When I saw Hank's even and quick swing, I decided his style was for me. He had great wrist timing, and for the rest of that summer I copied his style and stance. I wasn't able to hit the ball as far as Thompson did, but I was spraying a lot of line drives.

It turned out that someone had been watching me play during this time, particularly when we were in Dallas. He was Bill Blair, a former pitcher-outfielder for the Indianapolis Clowns. He was playing and scouting for the Detroit Colts, a Negro touring team based in Amarillo, Texas.

After seeing me play a few softball games, Blair told my father, "I think your son has a future in baseball—if he can play that game as well as he plays softball."

Blair's observation pleased Dad, who had played with the Dallas Green Monarchs, a Sunday-holiday Negro baseball team. My dad liked to brag about his versatility. He had been the Green Monarchs' catcher when he wasn't pitching. My brother Benjamin and I had been the team's bat boys.

Before Blair came along, my parents had had a different outlook on my softball, based on the number of windows we broke whenever we played pepper in our backyard. Because tin was cheaper than glass, the Banks family had a lot of tin windows.

During my sophomore year in high school, Blair asked for my father's approval to arrange a baseball try-out for me. How could he place a skinny, seventeen-year-old softball shortstop in baseball? We all wondered.

Surprisingly, Blair came up with an answer. He arrived at our house with Johnny Carter, the owner-manager of the Detroit Colts, and the entire neighborhood buzzed with excitement.

Carter was driving a brand-new Dodge. It was the newest and most expensive automobile I had ever seen. While everybody wanted to know who were the rich folks visiting the Banks, I had a different idea. All I wanted to do was drive that car around the block!

Carter was so well dressed that you would have thought he was a model who had just stepped out of a Neiman-Marcus window display. I had never been inside the store, but I had walked past it enough times, wishing I owned some of the suits, topcoats, shirts and ties on display.

Finally, the decision to allow me to go to Amarillo to try out was left to my mother. She approved, saying, "I'm all for Ernest doing anything he wants to do in sports just as long as it doesn't interfere with his schooling. His finishing high school comes first, ahead of anything else."

Both Blair and Carter promised her I would be home in plenty of time to return to high school that fall. To make sure that I would have company, Carter also made an offer to a friend of mine, Marvin Hickman. Marvin's parents approved on the same grounds that mine did. While we were trying out, the Colts would pay for our lodging and meals.

Early in the morning three days later Blair and Carter picked me up. I was in the clouds. That new Dodge was outside, and I was going to ride in it. What's more, I was actually going to try out with the Detroit Colts.

It's 319 miles as the crow flies from Dallas to Amarillo. Within an hour, I was looking out at parts of Texas I had never seen before. Marvin rode in the back seat with me, and about halfway to Amarillo, I was suddenly scared and nervous. This would be the first time I had been away from home overnight and the first time I would stay in a hotel. I leaned back in the seat and tried to sleep—something I've always been able to do, even standing up in a telephone booth—but I was just too nervous. Apparently Blair and Carter sensed my uneasiness, and in an effort to calm me down they told one story after another about their baseball experiences.

When we finally reached Amarillo, Carter drove to the Mount Olive Hotel in the Negro section of the city and signed us in on a big ledger. The clerk gave us a key to room 24, on the second—and top—floor. Marvin raced me up the long stairs to our room. We opened the door and saw two beds with mattresses that curved like rainbows and an old dresser. By today's standards the room was pretty dismal, but it looked like a palace to us.

Marvin flicked on the lights, and we felt like a couple of young millionaires as we unpacked our clothes. Besides underwear and socks, each of us had brought along a spare pair of pants, an extra sweater and two extra shirts—our entire wardrobes.

Looking at those freshly made beds, we decided to take a nap, but Marvin said he couldn't go to sleep until we had made a little wager. He wanted to bet me a dollar he would be a better second baseman for the Colts than I would be a shortstop. I didn't have the dollar, but I accepted the bet.

Mr. Blair woke us up for supper. We ate in a nearby nightclub where Carter had arranged for us to just sign the check without paying for the dinner. I learned later that this was easy for Carter to do since he owned the club as well as the Colts.

During the dinner I sat next to Marvin, and everything he said, I repeated. (I figured he knew all the right things to do since his father owned a club in Dallas.) Marvin ordered chicken and all the trimmings and two bottles of Coke. I ordered the same things. Although I preferred milk, I was too bashful to say so.

While we ate, the Colts' big pitcher, Frank Barnes, came over to our table and said he would be glad to help us out in any way he could. When he said the Colts needed some younger players and that he hoped we would both make the club, we finally began to relax.

Back in our hotel room, we turned off the lights and jumped into bed, thoroughly exhausted. But before I could close my eyes, Marvin yelled, "Ernie, look at the far corner of the ceiling and tell me what you see." My first reaction was that this was a gag because I didn't think it was possible for a hotel room to have a hole that big in the ceiling.

"They must think we're two new stars," I said to Marvin, "because they gave us the starlight room. We can see stars without looking out the window."

The next morning Blair called us for breakfast. Afterward, he ran us through the longest drill of my life. During that first day in Amarillo, we had an eight-hour workout, with Blair hitting fungoes to Marvin at second base and to me at shortstop. Boot one, and he would make the next two or three more difficult. This continued until late in the afternoon, but the day's work did not end then. Blair wanted to make sure we didn't have time to get homesick.

That night Blair conducted a baseball clinic, the first I had ever attended. He lectured us on the importance of fundamentals and playing heads-up baseball, on the signs the second baseman and shortstop should use on the double play or going into the outfield for the relay throw. Most of the Colts were from three to five years older than we were, and Blair wanted to make sure we would be able to handle the pace.

Blair repeated those double-duty sessions on our second and third day in camp. Our first day of real fun was the fourth. We spent most of it just hitting. Because the Colts didn't own a batting cage, we would hit for five minutes and then pick up baseballs for the next five.

The fourth night it rained, and the hole in the ceiling of our starlight room was no longer anything to joke about. The ceiling was so high we couldn't reach the hole without a stepladder. Little spots of water were forming pools on the floor, and our room was rapidly becoming a disaster area. I imagined the water causing a short in the electricity or flooding us out of the room altogether. I was wishing I were back home in Dallas when Marvin said, "I'm going downstairs and tell that room clerk to give us a new room, or we'll move out."

Move where? I asked myself.

Marvin bolted downstairs, talked to the clerk and there we were moving into a new room at 2 A.M.

Adversity stuck with us the next day. During practice, Marvin went back for a pop fly, fell and pulled a leg muscle. This kept him out of the season's first game the following day, and Carter moved Willie Jones to second base. When Carter read the lineups with my name as the starting shortstop I was more shook than confident.

About five hundred people turned out for the game, and I was so edgy I'm sure I heard every word that was spoken in the stands. As we took the field, I gave myself pep talks and tried to recall all the signs and signals Blair had taught us earlier. I missed Marvin. In fact, I had never felt so much alone.

The pitching on both sides was good, and it was still a scoreless game when I came up to bat for the third time. Swinging at a belt-high fast ball, I hit a drive to left-center. Aided by a convenient wind blowing out from the plate, the ball dropped over the fence for a home run.

It was the proudest moment of my life. I doffed my cap as I crossed the plate with Blair coming to greet me.

I had no idea what he meant when he yelled, "Get up in the stands and pass your cap." Quickly he explained, "It's the custom for a player to go into the stands after he's hit a home run and pass his cap. That way the fans are able to show their appreciation of his achievement."

I took the cue in a hurry, and the fans responded with pennies, nickels, dimes and a few quarters. I returned to the field at the inning's end and poured the coins into the pocket of my jacket. After the game, Blair and Marvin helped me count the loot—six dollars and some change. I had never made money so easily and so quickly.

We played in Amarillo again the next day, and I'm sure you can guess what I was doing: swinging for the fences! The wind wasn't as cooperative, however, and I didn't get to pass my cap again.

After that second game, Carter told me I had made the team and would be leaving with the Colts the next morning on their first trip. The Colts' schedule wasn't too elaborate, but we visited other cities in Texas and places in Kansas, Oklahoma, Nebraska and New Mexico, playing small-town teams at almost every stop.

By now it was obvious why Carter drove that new Dodge and dressed so well. Besides owning the Colts and the nightclub in Amarillo, he also booked famous black dance bands and entertainers into most of the cities we visited. Carter's name was magic in those small towns. Whenever our bus broke down—and that was pretty often—his friends would round up enough automobiles to carry us to the next town. When restaurants and hotels weren't available, we would split up and lodge with black families in the towns we were visiting. Carter seemed to know everybody everywhere, and it was during this trip that I learned the full impact of "Johnny Carter sent me."

In some of the bigger cities the parks were larger, and our baseball games were often followed by rodeos. I had never seen a rodeo and was intrigued by the roping acts. Sometimes I borrowed a rope from one of the cowboys and tried to duplicate their feats, all the time with two feet on the ground. I love horses, but riding in a rodeo wasn't for me!

Carter never overlooked an opportunity to promote his attractions. Whenever we moved into a new city or town, especially during the second half of the season, we would see big placards reading:

> Come out and see Marvin Hickman and Ernie
> Banks, the Detroit Colts' two new, young stars
> from Dallas.

Me a star? I didn't believe it but that's what the signs said.

My first season ended in Hastings, Nebraska, where we played Owen's All-Stars before the largest crowd of the year. The fans had flocked to Hastings from all the surrounding towns and countryside just to see Mickey Owen. One of the major leagues' original jumpers to the outlaw Mexican League, Owen was under suspension when he formed this All-Star team.

I don't remember the outcome of the game, but I do know I earned more that day than I ever had. My share of the Colts' percentage split was $12.50. What a way to close out the season—going home with $12.50, and it was all mine until I reached Dallas. In Dallas the money would go to my mother who would decide the best way to spend it.

During that summer when I was away from home, my mother took a part-time job at the Dallas Medical Center and earned enough money to have our home wired for electricity. We paid twenty dollars a month rent, but that didn't include the luxury of electric lights. It was an event to be remembered when we switched from lamps to electricity, and it meant I had one less daily chore. I didn't have to carry the kerosene to keep the lamps filled anymore.

When school reopened I reported for football, and

I spent more time at the YMCA. We still couldn't afford a membership, but the instructors always welcomed us into the gym. The baseball tour with the Colts had heightened my interest in softball, but it didn't seem as much fun playing the game indoors.

That fall Coach Hollie converted me to a two-way football player, halfback on offense and end on defense. I also played basketball, practicing outdoors on the campus and playing our home games at the YMCA.

Blair had already told my parents I was wanted back for a second season with the Colts. With school, football, basketball and softball, my junior year literally flew by.

Things were different my second summer in Amarillo. I had lost Marvin as my roommate; he had quit, discouraged over his troublesome leg injury. Now I felt a genuine acceptance among my older teammates; they treated me as a member of the team, not just another kid player. I didn't have to worry about a hole in the ceiling of my hotel room, or the "let the kid do it" chants of the older players when there was an errand to be run or an odd job to be done.

I was determined to bear down and really improve my game. I was Ernie Banks, shortstop for the Detroit Colts, and I was not about to let anyone question it.

2

Monarchs

While I was traveling with the Colts, I ran into "Cool Papa" Bell, an outstanding black player. Several times "Cool Papa" compared notes with Blair about my potential, and I'm sure the Kansas City Monarchs learned about me through this Bell-Blair pipeline. After I had finished my second season with the Colts, the Monarchs —at that time the Yankees of black baseball—sent two of their representatives to my home.

Barney Sorrell and Dizzy Dismukes discussed my future with my parents and after this meeting Mr. and Mrs. Eddie Banks knew two things: Their oldest son had just one year to go to receive his high school diploma, and he had a job waiting for him after that. I suspect that they had trouble believing their ears when Sorrell and Dismukes told them my starting salary would be $300 a month if I signed with the Monarchs and, of course, if I made the club. This was big, big money to two people who had worked hard all their lives and never even come close to earning $300 a month.

That fall I captained the football team, earning my second letter. As a senior, I also lettered in basketball. I also reported to the track team, trying for a third letter that year, but my dashing speed has never carried me too far too fast. I competed in the broad- and high-jumping events, but I didn't get that letter.

The day after graduation I was on a bus to Kansas City, arriving just in time to attend a banquet honoring the Monarchs. All the players were asked to say a few words, and when they called on me all I could say was, "Thank you. I'm happy to be here, and I hope to make the team."

Very few fans today realize what a flourishing concern Negro baseball was during the 1930s and 1940s. There were sixteen organized teams divided into two eight-team leagues, the Negro American and the Negro National leagues. Each fall the two league champions competed in the Negro World Series.

The Negro American League had the Birmingham Black Barons, Chicago American Giants, Cincinnati Crescents, Cleveland Buckeyes, Indianapolis Clowns, Kansas City Monarchs, Memphis Red Sox and St. Louis Stars. The Negro National League consisted of the Baltimore Elites, Brooklyn Royals, Detroit Stars, Homestead (Pennsylvania) Grays, Newark Eagles, New York

Cubans, Philadelphia Stars and Pittsburgh Crawfords.

Buck O'Neil, my manager with the Kansas City Monarchs, and Tom Baird, the Monarchs' owner, were among the pioneers who helped organize these leagues. By the time I got to the Monarchs in 1950, some of the clubs had disbanded, drained of their young, topflight players after Jackie Robinson broke the color line with the Brooklyn Dodgers.

During the heyday of Negro baseball, Satchel Paige and Josh Gibson, a slugging catcher, were two of the most famous players. I played with Paige when he pitched for the Monarchs, and I still haven't figured out how anybody could hit his hesitation pitch. Old-timers still call Gibson the Negro Babe Ruth of his era. They say Josh was so powerful he could hit a baseball over any fence in any park—and he frequently did.

Paul Hardy, who is now in his thirty-first season working in the Chicago office of the Harlem Globetrotters basketball team, recalls that Jim Gilliam was the bat boy when he caught for the Nashville (Tennessee) Elites. The Elites, Hardy claims, actually launched franchise moving when the Elites left Nashville and set up shop in Washington, D.C. After a year in Washington, the Elites moved to Baltimore and became one of the most famous teams in Negro baseball. Hardy's successor as catcher for the Elites was a man named Roy Campanella. Campy joined the Baltimore club in 1936.

Teams like my first one, the Detroit Colts based in Amarillo, Texas, played semipro ball without any league affiliations. The Monarchs traveled all over the country, but the Colts just moved from city to city playing town and industrial teams.

Besides owner Tom Baird and manager John "Buck" O'Neil, who later became a successful scout-coach for the Chicago Cubs, Curt Roberts, who moved up to the Pittsburgh Pirates, and Elston Howard, who later coached for the New York Yankees after an outstanding playing career with the Bronx Bombers, also became my friends when I joined the Monarchs.

Some of the younger Monarchs, like myself, had just finished high school. Others were enrolled in college and spent the summer playing with the club. My first impression of the Monarchs was that, young or old, there was great warmth between the players and the management.

The day after the banquet I played my first Monarchs game at shortstop against the Indianapolis Clowns in Blues Stadium—then the home of the Kansas City Blues in the American Association. I had never seen a park as big as that one, much less played in one. I was nineteen years old and I was nervous—even more nervous than on that first day in Amarillo.

When we reached the clubhouse O'Neil read us a time schedule for the warm-up. Everything was measured to the minute, so much time for hitting, so much for infield practice, and so on. All I wanted was to look around and get the feel of everything, the well manicured green grass, the big advertising signs on the outfield fences, the huge dugouts complete with water fountains and the massive stands.

I warmed up playing catch with Bill Breeden. He represented something special to me. Bill was a student at Southern University, the school my later Cubs' teammate Lou Brock attended. Bill was articulate and I learned a lot listening to him talk.

When it was time for infield drill Buck sounded as if he were calling off the names of four astronauts about to launch a trip to the moon. "Cooper to first, Roberts to second, Banks to shortstop and Baldy Sewell to third!" he yelled.

During this drill Roberts explained the signs we would use covering second. As Curt spoke, I recalled Blair's teachings during my first season in Amarillo. Baseball really was a science.

After we returned to the dugout, the Clowns began their shadow ball infield drill. It was all pretense, everybody faking catching and throwing the ball in every way imaginable. The fans ate it up, and so did a rookie named Ernie Banks.

When the grounds crew began dragging and raking the infield, Buck, who had come over to sit beside me in the dugout, explained what was going on. "They are dragging the infield, and once they finish, they will water it down to assure the best playing surface possible. They do it in all major-league and most of the bigger minor-league parks."

"Playing on a field that smooth, a player should never boot one," I said to Buck.

He laughed and answered, "In theory you are absolutely right. A player should never kick one. But just wait, it happens to everybody—even you—if you play long enough."

Finally we took the field. I had the kind of jitters that are hard to describe. It was like being closed in with ten thousand people just staring right down on you. Curt Roberts reminded me of our signs: When he covered his face with his glove, he would cover second, and when he touched his chin with his glove, I would cover. Then he hollered, "Relax!"

It was impossible. The tension, I found out, affected my timing at the plate. I made contact with the ball all three times, but I was swinging late and flied out to right field each time.

When the game was over, Buck said, "Young man, you made a fine start. You hit the ball well three different times. Just speed up your swing a bit and the ball will start falling in. Stay loose, forget the tension and you'll be all right."

Most of our travel was aboard the Monarchs' own bus, and we were paid from $3 to $5 a day for meals, depending on the city or town in which we played. After that first game against the Indianapolis Clowns we cut out of Kansas City and headed for Memphis, Birmingham, Atlanta and Chattanooga before going into Florida.

After finishing in Florida, we worked our way up the Atlantic Coast to New England and then into Pennsylvania, Ohio, Michigan and other midwestern states. I learned a lot of geography on those trips and I learned a lot more about major-league baseball by reading the newspapers in the larger cities.

When we reached Chicago, and I watched the Cubs playing on a Wednesday afternoon on television, I was surprised. Until then, I had just taken it for granted that the major leagues played the same kind of schedule as the Monarchs—night games during the week and daylight doubleheaders on Sundays and holidays. Afternoons in Chicago were something to look forward to when the Cubs were playing at home.

On the Monarchs' bus I usually sat with Elston Howard or Gene Richardson. Elly's theories about baseball were the most interesting I had heard. In my book, he earned the right to be called a pro while still playing for the Monarchs.

The Monarchs' schedule was built around Negro clubs, such as the Memphis Red Sox, the Birmingham Black Barons and the Indianapolis Clowns. We would play one team ten or twelve straight games and then switch off to new opposition. Now and then we played in major-league parks, but more often we used a specific park in the black districts of the larger cities.

To make some of the longer trips on schedule, we had to drive nonstop. We stocked up on lunch meat, bread, crackers, cookies, candy bars and soda pop, but if you made the mistake of falling asleep before eating, the chances were you'd go hungry. Some of the best knife-and-fork men I've ever met played for the Monarchs, and most of them took added pleasure in eating a teammate's lunch.

Whenever a player "donated" his lunch to his teammates and was tapioca—without funds—to boot, Buck would give him a lecture on guarding his possessions and a dollar "touch" to buy new supplies. O'Neil had tremendous rapport with his players, and he always had the right answers to cure everything from homesickness to hitting slumps.

Duke Henderson was an outstanding outfielder, but he often threatened to jump the club and go home. Buck would listen to him, and just before Duke was ready to make his move, Buck would call Henderson's home and have Duke talk to his parents. That would be the last you would hear about Henderson leaving—until the next time he got homesick.

Most baseball men, especially scouts, held both Baird and O'Neil in high esteem. Wherever we went we would see scouts huddling with them, listening to their evaluations of players, those playing for other black teams as well as those playing for the Monarchs.

During my first season Elston Howard was sold to the New York Yankees, who assigned him to Muskegon, Michigan, in the Central League. After Howard left, I remember Gene Richardson saying, "With his great potential and competitive fire, Elly will be catching for the Yankees a long, long time." Gene was right. Howard caught more than sixteen hundred games during fourteen major-league seasons.

During the last month of the Monarchs' season, Buster Hayward, the catcher-manager of the Indianapolis Clowns, asked if I would get in touch with him before I returned to Dallas. I had no idea what it was all about, but I took Buster's telephone number and promised I would call. When I did, the first thing Hayward asked was, "How would you like to make a month's tour with Jackie Robinson's Major League All-Stars and the Clowns?"

I was flabbergasted, but Buster kept right on talking. "Jackie is organizing an All-Star team to be built around himself, Roy Campanella, Don Newcombe and Larry Doby. His team will tour for a month after the World Series is completed, playing against the Clowns. If you're interested, just show up in Jacksonville, Florida, within three days. That's where the tour starts, and I'll fill you in on the rest of the details when you get there."

Buster didn't say anything about salary and I forgot to ask. It wouldn't have made any difference; I'd have played for nothing. Except for the Monarchs' original offer of $300 a month, money really hasn't meant that much to me. That first offer was staggering, to my parents as well as myself. Since then I just haven't considered it a baseball versus money situation—especially when the big dollar is weighed against the personal pleasure of playing ball.

I called my mother and told her I would be a month late getting home. She was disappointed, but I knew she was as thrilled as I was when she heard I was going to tour with Jackie Robinson's Major League All-Stars. She just told me to go ahead, keep in touch and let her know how things were going.

Jeff Williams, an outfielder for the Clowns, offered me a ride to Jacksonville. We took turns at the wheel and arrived there a day ahead of schedule, which was a break since the Yankees had swept the World Series from the Phillies in four straight games, and a lot of the players were already in Jacksonville.

Hayward arranged for me to room with Williams in a hotel in the black section of Jacksonville, and the next morning we were all introduced to Jackie Robinson. Jackie's words were music to my ears.

"Banks, we'll use you at shortstop on an alternating basis. One game you'll play for the Clowns and the next game you'll play for the All-Stars. We'll do a lot of shifting to assure everybody playing time."

Again I was living in a dream world. I was going to be playing alongside Jackie Robinson, on the same team with Campanella, Newcombe and Doby.

The tour got off to a terrific start. Newcombe pitched some great shutout innings, and Campy proved why he was a leading catcher. During a game in Memphis, Tennessee, Doby hit one of the longest home runs I had ever seen. The ball sailed out of the park like a rocket. It was truly a tape-measure job.

We didn't see any of the major leaguers away from the playing field. They either flew or drove their own cars from game to game, while the Clowns traveled by bus.

Before a game in Meridian, Mississippi, I was standing around the batting cage looking and learning as usual when Jackie Robinson walked up to me. "Young man," he said, "I've been watching you, and you really can pull that inside pitch. You hit very well."

It was the greatest compliment I had ever had from a super star. A few days later he took me aside and said, "You're too slow getting rid of the ball. One split second could cost a double play. I'd suggest you learn to release the ball faster."

He also stressed the importance of a shortstop giving the ball to the second baseman high enough so that he could make the throw to first base without any lost motion.

During the game that very day a grounder was hit to me in the hole at shortstop. I pounced on it, threw quickly to Robinson at second, and he turned it into a double play.

"Now you've got it!" he yelled.

When the tour reached Dallas, my folks came to the park. They were thrilled to see me play with major leaguers, and their excitement doubled when I introduced them to Jackie, Campy, Larry and Newk after the game. The four of them took turns complimenting me on my good play on the tour, and my father smoked two cigars during the time it would normally take him to smoke one.

Our tour ended a week later. Hayward paid me $400 and expenses for the month. I didn't say much more than "thank you" to Buster before I ran straight to the nearest clothing store. I bought a bright red shirt and sweater and a pair of pearl gray slacks and changed clothes right there in the store. Then I caught a train for Dallas, deciding to leave the bus to the driver.

I took a cab home and felt like a millionaire, giving the driver a five-dollar bill and telling him to keep the change. Inside the house I tossed the wad of bills on the dining-room table and yelled, "We're rich!"

My father's eyes sparkled. "God Almighty, son, you are rich," he said. "I've never seen that much money, and look at you—you are really dressed for high society."

One by one my buddies showed up at the house as word got around that I had returned. Rastein Goodson came early. Our families were good friends, and even though he had dropped out of school, we had kept in touch. Rastein suggested we see a movie. He said a good Western was playing at the Harlem, and although I wasn't in a movie mood, when he kept asking, I gave in. On the way, it was quickly obvious that Rastein wasn't in a movie mood either. What he really wanted was for me to help him get his watch out of hock.

Despite my pleading that the money belonged to my parents, Rastein got me inside the pawnshop and we made a three-way trade at my expense. Rastein gave me his pawn ticket. I put $15 with it and gave both to the broker, who returned the watch to Rastein. I've met some fast talkers but that time Rastein could have sold me the Brooklyn Bridge. Even though I realized I would never again see my $15, I had to laugh at Rastein's jive.

On the way home I stopped at the neighborhood drugstore, where we usually hung out. A lot of familiar faces were missing, and finally it dawned on me why— they were in the service. At nineteen, soon to be twenty, I realized my turn might be coming soon.

3

Letter from
the President

Several weeks later I received a letter with greetings
from the President of the United States. I had a date for
my service physical examination.

After passing the physical, I was one of fifty men
from the Dallas area to report to the induction center.
From there we bussed to Fort Sill, Oklahoma. I hardly
had time to stretch my legs before a businesslike sergeant tapped me on the shoulder and said I had been
assigned to KP duty. That was fine with me, I told
him, but exactly what was KP?

It didn't take me long to learn. Kitchen Patrol
ended at midnight, and the next day I was on the move
again, this time bound for Fort Bliss, Texas, for basic
training. At Fort Bliss I was assigned to the 45th AAA
Gun Battalion. After a briefing session, the lights were

turned out. It really wasn't necessary; I could have slept with them all on.

The next morning I couldn't get out of my bunk. My left knee had locked, and it hurt when I put the slightest weight on it. Most of the fellows in our battalion kidded me, claiming I was trying to "jake" it. After I had convinced them I couldn't dress or walk, the sergeant put me on sick call. Preliminary examinations failed to locate the trouble, so they moved me to William Beaumont Army Hospital in a jeep.

There one of the doctors mentioned that an operation might be necessary. I almost jumped out of my skin—in the Army three days and already on the operating table!

After more examinations, the doctors ordered complete bed rest and the use of weights to stretch the leg. I stayed in bed for two weeks. The third week they had me up again to walk and test the knee, but the condition was unchanged and I was ordered back to bed.

A restless week later one of the doctors said, "You look athletic. We have a hospital unit softball team for the doctors, and it might be good therapy if you worked out with our team."

The idea was good, but I still couldn't put any weight on the knee, so it was back to bed with the weights. Eight days later they got me up again. This time the leg seemed as good as new and I returned to my battalion to start training.

I went through every phase of training without any pain or trouble. We didn't actually fire antiaircraft guns at Fort Bliss but we spent considerable time on simulated drills and maneuvers. I was a cannoneer, the second of three men on a line passing ammunition to a man who charged it and put it in the gun.

Our battalion was composed mostly of young blacks from Texas, Alabama and Mississippi. They picked me as flag bearer for the squad, which was almost like being elected captain.

Long after finishing basic training I received a phone call from the late, great Goose Tatum. The Harlem Globetrotters had a game booked in nearby El Paso that night, and Tatum said Abe Saperstein, the Trotters' owner-coach, had suggested that I might be interested in being a part-time player for this game. I was on my way to El Paso before Goose could hang up.

I reported immediately to the auditorium, and the first person I met was Marcus Haynes, the famous dribbler. Marcus knew some of my baseball teammates with the Colts and the Monarchs and we talked over old times. Saperstein arrived a bit later, welcomed me and gave me a uniform and other equipment. He also briefed me on the game plan, saying how he planned to use me —a few minutes in both halves.

When the game started Saperstein said: "Sit here next to me, and I'll describe our plays to you. That way you'll know what to do when I put you in."

This may seem unbelievable, but that's exactly what happened. I'd never sat next to a white man, and I wasn't sure what to do. Abe repeated his words, and I finally moved. Then the antics of the Globetrotters got me laughing and I relaxed. In the game I missed my first shot, an easy lay-up, and Goose clowned on the sidelines. After the game Abe took all the players out for dinner and invited me to go along. It was a great party. Saperstein later arranged for my transportation back to Fort Bliss, paid for that and also gave me a good game fee.

My playing with the Trotters was big news at the Fort. The next morning at breakfast one of my buddies said, "Finally, we know who you are—a Harlem Globetrotter. Ernie, the Trotter!"

Try as I might, I still couldn't convince him baseball was my game and that I was merely a run-of-the-mill basketball player. What they didn't know, and I didn't talk about it, is that sports had given me my first opportunity to sit next to a white man—and he happened to be someone as important as Abe Saperstein, the legendary liberal who helped so many young black athletes in baseball and basketball.

Our official marching orders said to report to New Orleans, Louisiana, January 25, 1952, for overseas duty. I spent a twenty-one-day furlough at home and then headed for New Orleans to rejoin my battalion.

The seventeen-day trip across the Atlantic to Bremerhaven should have been made on a hospital ship— everybody was that sick, including me. The Pilgrims couldn't have been any happier to reach Plymouth Rock than we were to reach Bremerhaven.

From Bremerhaven we moved to Mittenthal in the Alps, and it was tempting to goof off. I did and I was quickly assigned to KP duty.

I was busy with my pots and pans when an order came through for baseball candidates to sign up. I didn't hear about this, but a buddy, Ronald Gilmore, who knew I had played with the Kansas City Monarchs, put my name on the list.

Early in April the candidates were ordered to report to Mannheim. We were housed in the 95th Gun Battalion barracks in Mannheim, and Sergeant Davis ordered everybody to report for a noon drill the next day. From KP duty to a noon assignment—in the Army that's unbelievable!

When we saw so many good players assembled, Chick Greenwood, a Chicagoan I had gotten to know and like, suggested, "We'd better have a little talk to get our signals straight. The talent here is pretty good, and we don't want to miss out by overmatching ourselves."

We had heard through the grapevine that Don Akins, a second baseman, Hal Wadsworth, a shortstop, and Jim Price, an outfielder, were among the best players in camp. Chick knew Price's favorite position was left field, so he went out for right field. During that first drill Greenwood looked outstanding, and Sergeant Davis was heard to say, "This Greenwood looks like a complete player. I'm going to start him in right."

Now it was established that Chick was set, but what about me? Davis worked me at second base, but it wasn't one of my better days. I was rusty, and I felt out of place working on the wrong side of the base. My hitting was better than my fielding and saved me when the selections were completed.

The squads were filled for a six-team league tied to a split season to assure a championship series between the first- and second-half winners at the season's end. Our Mittenthal team got off to a blazing start.

We played a few games before I was finally moved to shortstop. Right after the switch from second to short I had a 5-for-5 game in Ossoburg: two singles, two doubles and a triple. When I returned to the clubhouse a sportswriter from *Stars & Stripes* was waiting to talk to me. He congratulated me on my hitting and said he wanted to check out a rumor from the States that the Cleveland Indians were interested in signing me. It was news to me. I told him the only person I knew in the Cleveland organization was Larry Doby, and I had only met him during my month's tour with the Jackie Robinson All-Stars after the 1950 season. That far from home, it was very pleasant to think that Doby might have recommended me to the Indians.

When we got back to Mittenthal, there was a letter from Bill Veeck inviting me to try out with the Indians after I finished my military duty. There was also a letter from Fresco Thompson, a farm-system executive for the Brooklyn Dodgers. He invited me to try out with the Dodgers after my Army stint. All I could think of was that Larry Doby and Jackie Robinson both had decided that my tour playing had earned me tryouts with their organizations. From then on I read *The Sporting News* each week, checking the progress of both the Dodgers and Indians in the box scores.

A string of key injuries cost our Mittenthal team the first-half championship. We were lucky to finish second. During the second half, more injuries and the loss of several players who had finished their tours of duty forced us to finish out of contention in fifth place. However, the season wasn't without a personal reward. President Eisenhower ordered all branches of the services integrated, and I was promoted to NCO Athletic Director in our company headquarters.

My first job was to organize a football team. I drafted my buddy Chick Greenwood as the No. 1 choice.

Some weeks later I was grounded again. My knee locked just as it had at Fort Bliss, and I was back in bed with more weights attached to my leg. The only compensation I got for being bedridden was that I was able to listen to every play of the 1952 World Series between the Brooklyn Dodgers and the New York Yankees.

The games were carried on the Armed Forces Overseas Radio Network, and I felt a little let down when the Yankees won in seven games. I was still looking forward to a tryout with the Dodgers.

After three weeks the leg was working again, and I returned to my duties as Athletic Director. I had two new projects, first to organize a basketball team and then a boxing team. The assignments were eye-openers. I had accepted the Army baseball program as a matter of course, but the interest in football and basketball and boxing amazed me. All these men wanted to compete even if it meant surrendering their off-duty time!

Christmas so far from home was a lonely time, but my blues were tempered by the knowledge that my overseas duty would end in mid-January. I did some traveling with the basketball and boxing units and this helped me feel less lonely too.

Anxious as I was to get back stateside, I found it difficult to say good-bye to my buddies. I left with a list of telephone calls as long as my arm to make to relatives and friends of these soldier-athletes when I reached home.

It had taken seventeen days to go over, but we returned in nine. The trip gave me time to think about my future; I wanted it to be in baseball, that was for sure.

We passed the Statue of Liberty and the New York skyline, and after disembarking were sent to Camp Kilmer, New Jersey. I moved from Camp Kilmer to Fort Sill, where my official discharge was finalized March 8, 1953.

I wasn't home in Dallas more than a day or two when I put in a call to Buck O'Neil. I finally reached him in Atlanta, and before I had an opportunity to ask if I still had a job with the Kansas City Monarchs, he said, "We're training here in Atlanta. I have a new uniform out and hanging in a locker. When can I expect you to report?"

Good old Buck hadn't forgotten me! I reached the Monarchs' camp two days later.

I was so anxious to get going in baseball I didn't even take the time to check out the tryout letters I'd received the previous summer from the Cleveland Indians and Brooklyn Dodgers. They were great morale boosters when I was so far away from home, but now all my thoughts centered around just one thing: returning to the Monarchs and Buck.

Actually I had forgotten all about the two tryout offers before I called Buck, and apparently the Indians and Dodgers were so busy at that particular time filling their minor-league club rosters they had forgotten about me.

Considering everything, it's probably just as well the situation worked out as it did. Pee Wee Reese was still going strong for the Dodgers, and the Indians were breaking in a new shortstop named George Strickland they had secured from the Pittsburgh Pirates.

With players like Reese and Strickland, I don't think either club was too concerned about working out an untested rookie named Ernie Banks.

All my life I have been blessed with older persons to guide and encourage me. Buck was one of the most important, along with Woody Culton, Coach Hollie, J. W. Worlds, Bill Blair, Johnny Carter, Abe Saperstein and Tom Baird.

Reading that Abe Saperstein had been voted into basketball's Hall of Fame in January 1971 made me very happy. "Uncle Abe," as I called him—as so many of his athletes did—played a very special part in my life when he provided me with my first chance to play with the Harlem Globetrotters in El Paso, when I was stationed at Fort Bliss.

You never forget such kindness, and now I have a very special reason for wanting to visit basketball's famous shrine in Springfield, Massachusetts. He did a lot to help improve the black athlete's status in basketball all around the world.

4

Yellow Laces
Are for Hot Dogs

There were a lot of new, young players with the Monarchs. Right away Buck told us about organized baseball's increased interest in black players and our entire squad began dreaming of the big time.

After a week of training, we spent a week playing in the Atlanta area. Buck would point out major-league scouts in the stands from time to time. Some were great players I had read about who had retired and turned to scouting. Buck never had to stress the importance of hustle or the need for heads-up baseball, every game, every day. With the scouts watching it was automatic with all of us.

On our second trip into Chicago that season we spent the night at the Pershing Hotel on the South Side before going to Muskegon, Michigan, the next day. After

64

supper I was sitting in the lobby watching television when Buck came over to me.

"Get hold of Bill Dickey," he said, "and the two of you meet me in the lobby at seven tomorrow morning."

Here we were in the last month of the season and Buck wanted us to meet him at 7 A.M. even though the bus wasn't scheduled to leave for Muskegon until noon. My first reaction was that he was kidding. Then I began to worry. Were we being sent home for one reason or another? Soon I lost all interest in watching television and went for a walk.

The next morning Dickey and I met Buck as scheduled. The three of us got into an automobile waiting in front of the hotel and drove off without a word of explanation from Buck. An hour later, the car stopped in front of Wrigley Field. Some men were working on a big electric sign outside the park.

Buck ushered us through a side door and up a short flight of stairs into the office of Wid Mathews. Tom Baird was sitting with Mathews and introduced him to Bill and me as the vice president of personnel for the Cubs.

Mathews was an enthusiastic and rapid talker. He was wearing a miniature red bow tie and I can remember how it bobbed up and down as he talked.

"The Chicago Cubs have arranged with Tom Baird to buy your contracts from the Kansas City Monarchs. Since the Monarchs aren't in organized baseball, we can't complete the deal until we receive your approval. Just answer yes or no."

I was hearing what the man said, but I wasn't believing it. Simply by saying one word—yes—we would become the property of a major-league baseball club. It was too good to be true. We both answered a very nervous "yes."

Mathews turned directly to Bill and said, "Our scouts feel you have a good chance as a right-handed pitcher in the major leagues. I'm offering you a Cedar Rapids [Iowa] contract for 1954. You will finish this season with the Monarchs and report to the Cedar Rapids club for spring training next March.

"The Cubs will send you a detailed conditioning program to follow this winter to assure your reporting to spring training in top physical shape. Our scouts and minor-league managers will check your progress, and you will be promoted as you prove yourself. Good luck."

Bill signed, and then Mathews turned to me.

"Banks, most of our scouts and some of our coaches are of the opinion that you are ready to play major-league baseball right now. In support of their opinion I am offering you a major-league contract. If you approve, we'll arrange with Baird and O'Neil to have you spend the next week playing with the Monarchs before reporting to us when the Cubs return to Wrigley Field.

"We'll give you a schedule indicating when you should return to Chicago. Our people will arrange to meet you at the airport and get a hotel reservation for you. Good luck, and don't get hurt in the meantime, because the Cubs have big money invested in you and Dickey."

I was so nervous I had to hold my right hand with my left as I scribbled Ernest Banks (Mathews asked me to use my first name instead of a nickname) on a document that seemed to be a mile long.

Baird stayed behind with Mathews as Buck escorted us back to the Pershing Hotel to pack for the trip to Muskegon. I had signed in such a hurry, I hadn't even noticed the salary figure. On the way back to the South Side, Buck kiddingly grabbed hold of my right arm so I wouldn't jump out of the automobile as he asked, "Do you realize that you signed for $800 a month? After your first full year in the majors, I want you to write me with news that your salary has been doubled. It's all up to you now."

That day turned out to be full of surprises. By the time we had returned to the Pershing, a Chicago sportswriter and a photographer were waiting for us. The photographer took a dozen pictures and the writer talked to us about our baseball experiences and our reactions to signing with the Cubs. I can't remember fully, but it had to be the shortest yes-and-no interview in the writer's experience. It was also the first time I realized how quickly a metropolitan newspaper picks up a lead.

On the way to Muskegon our bus buzzed with the news. Believe me, that old-time fellowship among the Monarchs really blossomed. Every man came up and shook our hands and offered congratulations.

In Muskegon Buck showed me a newspaper headline. It read:

Cubs Sign Monarchs'
Pitcher, Shortstop

The story, although not long, contained all the details and said I would report to the Cubs in a week to finish out the season, but the September 8, 1953, date on the sports page reminded me of something else. Just six months earlier, to the day, I had been discharged from the Army at Fort Sill. Now I was in Muskegon, Michigan, with my name on a major-league contract.

When I called home, I didn't have to tell my father the news. He had heard it on the radio. In his customary offhand manner, he said, "We are all very happy for you, son."

"Dad, my salary is $800 per month," I almost shouted back. "The first thing I'm going to do is buy you that automobile you've always needed."

At the ball park in Muskegon two more photographers wanted pictures of Bill and me. We posed for different shots and I could hear some fans, mostly kids, saying, "They must be the two players the Cubs signed." I wanted to climb on top of the dugout and shout the good news to the whole world.

After my last game with the Monarchs in Pittsburgh, I flew back to Chicago, following all the instructions Mathews had sent to Buck for me. Before I left the Monarchs' clubhouse, the players, one by one, came up to shake hands and wish me well. Sherwood Brewer advised, "The first thing you do after reporting to the Cubs is look up Ralph Kiner and introduce yourself."

Kiner, I told Sherwood, was a great home-run hitter and wouldn't want to be bothered by an untested rookie like me.

"Ralph is a good man. Make sure you get to know him because he'll help you," Brewer insisted.

Jeff Williams, who was with us when we made the tour with Jackie Robinson's Major League All-Stars, advised, "Remember just one thing; hustle. It's the number one demand in the majors. Make it your trademark and you'll end up earning a whole lot of money in the bigs."

It wasn't easy leaving those fellows. They were good friends, and I don't mind saying I made a moist-eyed trip to the Pittsburgh airport.

There are many stories about the cost of my move from the Kansas City Monarchs to the Chicago Cubs, and I think I eventually read all of them. Generally, two figures were mentioned. One story said the Cubs had paid the Monarchs $35,000 for both Bill Dickey and me. Another story set the figure at $50,000— $35,000 for me, and $15,000 for Dickey.

While any figure would be flattering to me, and I'm sure Bill would say the same, I never knew the whole story until I started to write this book. With assists from John Holland, vice president of the Cubs, and Gene Lawing, the Cubs' farm director, I finally know exactly how it all happened.

The Cubs paid $20,000 to the Monarchs for both Bill and me. At the Kansas City club's request, the Cubs made a down payment of $5,000 the day we signed, and the second payment of $15,000 was made January 10, 1954.

Like most players, unless they are top dollar bonus signees, I really never gave a thought to how much or how little the Cubs paid to secure me. However, I now know another story connected with my signing that means a great deal to me. It concerns Hank Aaron, a longtime friend, and Felix Mantilla, eventually one of my teammates on the Cubs.

In 1953, the Cubs had a working agreement with Macon, Georgia, a locally owned club in the Sally League. In the division of farm-system players, Solly Drake was to be optioned to Macon, where he would play center field, preparing for a future with the Cubs.

A few days before the Sally League season opened, Tom Gordon, the general manager who had been hired by the owners of the Macon club, called Lawing and expressed concern about whether Macon was ready to accept a Negro player.

Lawing immediately assigned Drake to Des Moines, and told Gordon he would send him the first available white outfielder to offset Solly's loss.

The Jacksonville, Florida, club, then a farm team for the Milwaukee Braves, wasn't as concerned about color as were the folks in Macon. Jacksonville fielded a team with Hank Aaron at second base and Felix Mantilla at shortstop.

A few weeks after the season opened, Jacksonville played in Macon and drew three straight sellout crowds with both Aaron and Mantilla playing. Gordon found his views changing with regard to the Negro player issue and called Lawing again, asking for Drake to be returned or another black player with Solly's talents to be assigned to Macon. Lawing had nobody to offer at the time and suggested that Gordon launch his own search.

"Where do I start?" Gordon asked.

Lawing answered that the all-black Kansas City Monarchs would be playing in Columbus, Georgia, the next night.

"Why don't you check out the Monarchs since they will be playing so close to you," Lawing said, "and discuss your situation with Tom Baird, who owns the Monarchs. He's a good friend of our organization and I'm sure he'll help you if he can."

Gordon scouted the game and singled me out as the new player he would like to have for the Macon club. In Columbus, he talked to Mr. Baird about buying my contract.

"Ernie Banks isn't for sale at this time," Baird said. "When he is, I'd like to deal directly with the Cubs or some other major-league club. That won't be for awhile. Not until we feel he's ready."

The next day Gordon repeated Baird's reply to Lawing over the telephone. That's what triggered the Cubs' interest in me.

Lawing sent a copy of the Monarchs' schedule to every Cubs' scout across the country with these instructions: Check out shortstop Banks when the Monarchs come into your territory, and give us a detailed game by game report of your findings.

While the scouts were divided in their rating of my chances as a twenty-two-year-old shortstop to make it in the majors, I had two boosters right from the start.

Ray Hayworth's report read:

Good accurate arm. Fielding ranges from good to outstanding. Sure hands. Moves well with good range right and left. Good running speed. Has good hitting form with quick wrists and level swing. Medium stride. A pull hitter.

Jimmy Payton filed his findings this way:

Throws well without lost motion. Really floats around shortstop and fields ball well from any position. Fast hands and recovers quickly. Could play any infield position. Will become good hitter. Doesn't swing at bad pitches.

When the Monarchs reached Chicago for some early September dates—the last one in Comiskey Park, the home of the White Sox—the Cubs sent two scouts for what Mathews and Baird agreed would be the last look before trying to make a deal.

Vedie Himsl, a longtime fixture in the Cubs' farm system, and Ray Blades, a former star outfielder with the St. Louis Cardinals, were picked to make the final assessment. Here is the combined Himsl-Blades report:

Good chance he is major leaguer right now.
Very good fielder with good hands and arm.
Good runner. Hustles well, and is good hitter
with power. Holds bat rather high, but drops
it when pitcher makes delivery. Does this fast
enough so we don't think it's a hitch. Out-
standing prospect.

Mathews met Baird for dinner that night at Chicago's Conrad Hilton Hotel, and worked out the deal— $10,000 for Dickey and $10,000 for Banks. They couldn't shake hands on the proposal until Lawing spelled out the agreement in baseball language since the Monarchs were an independent club and were not bound by the rules of organized baseball. This is why Bill and I signed with the Cubs as free agents after the Monarchs were paid for releasing us.

Where, I've often wondered, would I be now if Aaron and Mantilla hadn't disproved the idea that Macon wasn't ready to accept a Negro player?

When I landed in Chicago, a man introduced himself as Roy Johnson, a coach for the Cubs. What a start! I was being met by a major-league coach!

We talked only baseball during the drive from the airport to the Sheridan Plaza, where Johnson checked to see that my reservation was in order. I learned from Johnson that the Cubs had recalled Gene Baker from Los Angeles, and that Baker and I were to report the next day. We were the first Negroes eligible to play for the Cubs during the National League's championship season.

I welcome pressure, I said to myself as I looked around the lobby trying to recognize other players. I didn't see anyone, so I went to my room. Time moved slowly. I was too tense to sleep much. After rolling and tossing most of the night, I got up and dressed half an hour before I was to meet Johnson for breakfast.

While I waited in the lobby I spotted two men I was sure were players. There's a certain something about an athlete you usually don't miss. As we moved into the dining room Johnson introduced them to me as Frankie Baumholtz and Dee Fondy.

First I couldn't sleep. Now I couldn't eat. Johnson sensed my nervousness, so we picked up my gear and left. It was a very short drive to the field and when we got there Johnson said, "This is Wrigley Field, come with me."

I knew it was Wrigley Field; I had been there to meet Mr. Mathews. Nevertheless, the first walk into a major-league clubhouse as a player defies description. I was where I had always hoped to be—and I was petrified.

The Cubs' clubhouse was on the second level, reached by climbing a flight of stairs and taking a long walk along a railed ramp leading to the entrance. We were early, so there were only three Cubs for me to meet, Hank Sauer, Bill Serena and Randy Jackson.

The full impact of how my life had changed hit

me when Yosh Kawano, the Cubs' equipment manager, unpacked my gear. I noticed a big and sudden smile on his face, but what I didn't know until later was that he had spotted the bright yellow laces in my well-worn baseball shoes. Yosh disappeared quickly and returned with a pair of black laces in his hand. Speaking in almost a whisper, he said, "Maybe you ought to switch to these to conform with the rest of the fellows."

No big deal, just a friendly suggestion he shared only with me, proving his kindness and consideration. In baseball, at the major-league level, those bright yellow laces were for hot dogs. Yosh wanted to be sure I wouldn't be classed as one.

Yosh did me another favor, assigning me to a locker next to Hank Sauer. Hank used his home-run bat to earn the billing of "Mr. Mayor" with Wrigley Field fans.

After I had dressed for the game, Johnson escorted me down to the field. As we moved out of the clubhouse, Ralph Kiner arrived. I stopped while Johnson made the introductions. Ralph was as gracious as Sherwood Brewer had said he would be.

"It's good to know you," Ralph said, "and it's good having you with the Cubs. If there is anything I can do to help, just call on me."

What a great reception—meeting two home-run hitters like Hank Sauer and Ralph Kiner and having both of them say they were glad to meet me, me, Mr. Nobody from Dallas.

After an extended workout in the field, they called

me in to hit with the extra men. On the way to the batting cage I said to myself, "If you don't hit better than you field, they'll be sending you back to the Monarchs tomorrow night."

I spotted one of Ralph Kiner's R43 model bats on the ground outside the batting cage and asked him if he minded if I used it.

"Go right ahead," Ralph said, "but are you sure you like this model? What type are you used to?"

I had to tell him that where I came from we were happy to have bats, period. If a bat was new, you never worried about the model.

As I stepped into the Wrigley Field batting cage I was aware of the swarm of people around the cage. There were enough spectators to have made a big crowd for some of those softball games back in Dallas. With Johnson doing the throwing, I hit the first pitch into the left-field bleachers.

There was sort of a silence until Ralph Kiner yelled, "Hey, Banks, you can use all my bats if you promise to keep on hitting like that!"

I pulled a few more pitches into left, jogged around the bases and was called aside by the manager, Phil Cavarretta.

"I just watched you pull that pitch into the left-field seats," he told me. "Now I know why our scouts think so highly of you. Just take it slow and easy for a few days, and if there is anything I can do for you, let me know."

A bit later, Gene Baker showed up on the field.

His flight from Los Angeles had been delayed, so he was late getting to the park. He had bruised a muscle playing in his last game for the Los Angeles Angels and wasn't able to play immediately anyway.

In 1950 I had been Gene's replacement at short-stop for the Kansas City Monarchs, but we had never met. Watching all the individual Cubs rush to greet him gave me a warm feeling. He had been at spring training with the club earlier in the year, and everybody was glad to welcome him back.

Gene wasn't too mobile, but he took part in the second infield drill. Before we took the field, I asked him what signs we would use.

"Just watch me and everything will be all right. I'll tell you how to position yourself. Maybe we're both shortstops, but we'll get along."

Gene wasn't cocky, though he never lacked confidence in himself or his ability to help others. He helped me plenty.

That day the Cubs were playing the Brooklyn Dodgers. Before going to the dugout, I went over to talk to Jackie Robinson. Jackie asked: "Where's your home again?"

I said Dallas, and he answered, "Some great athletes come from Texas. I'm sure you'll live up to the true Texas tradition."

The Cubs beat the pennant-bound Dodgers, 3–1, behind Johnny Klippstein's outstanding pitching. It was the Cubs' tenth straight victory, and the clubhouse was a real fun palace. As I sat on the side watching all the antics, Gene yelled, "If you guys had played that way all season, we'd be where the Dodgers are!"

When I read about the Cubs' beating the Dodgers in the newspapers that night, my eyes focused on something else. There was my name in a headline which read:

Banks Hits "Homer"
on First Swing

Above the story was a picture of manager Phil Cavarretta welcoming the Cubs' first two Negro players —Baker and Banks. Within the hour, the story and the picture had been scissored out of the newspaper and were in the mail addressed to my parents in Dallas. It was their first newspaper clipping about their son as a full-fledged major leaguer.

The next day I saw Robin Roberts pitch for the first time. He beat the Cubs, 4–2, and hit a home run; Kiner and Sauer homered for the Cubs' only runs. The following day the Cubs made it eleven out of twelve by beating the Phillies, 7–4.

The fourth day I was already on the field when Cavarretta said what I had been wanting to hear.

"Ernie, you're in there today. You'll play shortstop and bat seventh behind Bill Serena. Good luck."

Curt Simmons, a famous lefty, was pitching for the Phillies. I asked Ralph Kiner for a rundown on Simmons' book of pitches and learned something very valuable about hitting.

"Don't worry too much about one particular pitch,"

Ralph advised. "Just go up there confident that you'll get your pitch and try to make contact. Hitting, good hitting, is confidence. Forget about his pitch and concentrate on getting your pitch."

The Phillies won the game, 16–4. I was 0-for-3 and made my first major-league error. It wasn't an impressive break-in, to say the least.

When a road trip with the Cubs took me to St. Louis, I could think of just one thing—getting to see Stan Musial. I got to the park early. It seemed as if Stan ran for a good half hour, and then he went into the batting cage and sprayed the ball to all the fields with exceptional power.

I got my first homer off Gerry Staley in a Sunday game against the Cardinals. It didn't do much to help the Cubs—we lost 11–6—but I was pleased about breaking the ice and seeing my name listed on the home-run line with such great hitters as Musial, Frankie Baumholtz and Red Schoendienst.

I played ten games for the Cubs before going home in the happiest of spirits. As I left my new teammates, I was feeling pretty good. Hank Sauer and Ralph Kiner shook hands with me. "Have a good winter," Hank said. "We'll be seeing you in spring training." And Ralph added, "Just keep on pulling the ball with those quick wrists and you won't need to worry about making it."

Again that good feeling—maybe, just maybe, I was on the verge of becoming a full-time major leaguer.

5

The Only Race
in Baseball

During my half-month stay with the Cubs in September 1953 I met more white people than I had known in all my twenty-two years. As a teen-ager in Dallas, I had lived in a black neighborhood, gone to school and associated with other blacks. That was simply our way of life, and it was no different with the first two ball teams I played for. The Detroit Colts was a Negro team. So was the Kansas City Monarchs, although their owner, Tom Baird, was white.

It's not easy even now to explain the fine relationships I had right from the beginning with all my teammates on the Cubs—and with such management people as Wid Mathews, Jimmy Gallagher, Gene Lawing, Phil Cavarretta, Roy Johnson and Bob Lewis. I have always been shy. The sudden association with so many white people often left me speechless and wondering why they were so kind.

Before we arrived in St. Louis on that first trip, Mr. Lewis, the Cubs' traveling secretary, reminded me several times to stick close to Gene Baker. I didn't understand why he was so worried until we walked through the big depot in St. Louis; there all the white players headed in one direction, to the Chase Hotel, while Gene and I took a cab to the Olive Hotel in the Negro section.

Fifteen minutes after we had reached our rooms, Gene had a telephone call from Mr. Lewis, checking to make sure everything was satisfactory and reminding us of the time to report for the game that night against the Cardinals in Sportsman's Park.

We lived like kings at the Olive: big beds, a big icebox filled with food and an insistent manager wanting to know if there was anything he could do to make our stay more enjoyable.

During our second day in St. Louis Gene suggested we kill some time seeing a movie. We hopped in a cab and drove around downtown until we finally picked out a show. But as we walked toward the ticket seller's booth, we could see her waving us away. Gene caught the significance of the wave, and as he turned away, he said, "I hope you enjoyed the show we aren't going to see at this theater." We took another cab back to the hotel and went to a show in the black neighborhood.

A couple of springs later my naïveté gave Gene a good laugh. Returning from the west, the Cubs stopped in New Orleans for several days. On one of those days we took a bus from New Orleans to Mobile for a game. When the bus stopped at one of the bigger hotels in Mobile, the white players got off to change into their uniforms. Manager Stan Hack told Gene and me he had arranged for us to dress at the ball park, and it would be best if we just waited on the bus.

I felt like taking a walk. Although Gene suggested I would be better off waiting in the bus, I left anyway. At the downtown bus station I walked into a store to buy a candy bar and a newspaper. Suddenly the owner rushed out from behind the counter, shouting a string of four-letter words and threatening to call the police if I didn't get out of there, and fast.

Needless to say, I left on the fly and hurried back to the Cubs' bus. Noting the expression on my face, Gene laughed overtime.

"I see you just learned the facts of life about southern hospitality."

A black-white situation worked just the reverse when the Cubs stopped in Beaumont, Texas. After the first game, one of the Chicago sportswriters came into the clubhouse and asked, "How are you going back to the hotel?"

After I kiddingly asked him "Yours or ours?" I said Mr. Lewis had ordered a taxi for us, and he was welcome to ride along.

When we walked out of the park with the white sportswriter, I could see that the black cabdriver was upset. He looked at me and said, "I could be arrested if I'm caught with a white passenger in my cab. I just can't carry that white man."

It took some doing, but after we promised to pay any fines he might incur, we got started. I'm sure the driver followed every back street in Beaumont on the way downtown. When we finally reached the business district, he stopped at the colored entrance to the bus station.

"This is as far as I can haul this white man. I just can't run the risk of losing my license, and that's what would happen if I'm caught."

Our disgruntled friend got out and walked the rest of the way to his hotel as we rode to ours. It's just as comedian George Gobel says: "You just can't hardly get that kind of service no more."

We ran into problems of segregation in the West, East and North as well as in the South. Shortly after the Giants moved from New York to San Francisco in 1958, the Cubs were in San Francisco for a weekend series. On Sunday morning the writer we had ridden with in Beaumont brought his wife to breakfast at the hotel where the Cubs were staying. As we talked across several tables, he noticed that my Cuban teammate Tony Taylor and I hadn't been served. Right away he invited us to move to his table and called the headwaiter over.

"This is Mr. Tony Taylor and this is Mr. Ernie Banks. They play for the Chicago Cubs. They are due at the ball park within the hour—and you wouldn't want them to play on empty stomachs, would you?"

That did it! Waiters were suddenly buzzing around our table. It turned out to be the last time I ever had to wait for food in San Francisco.

My philosophy about race relations is that I'm the man and I'll set my own patterns in life. I don't rely on anyone else's opinions. I look at a man as a human being; I don't care about his color.

Some people feel that because you are black you will never be treated fairly, and that you should voice your opinions, be militant about them. I don't feel this way. You can't convince a fool against his will. He is still going to hold to his opinions, so why should I tell him, "Look, you are prejudiced. You don't like me because I'm black." If a man doesn't like me because I'm black, that's fine. I'll just go elsewhere, but I'm not going to let him change my life. I don't think it's up to black athletes to get involved in political or racial issues. Our main objective should be to play whichever sports we are involved in and play well. We can't use prejudice as an excuse or as a crutch. In athletics, I feel, you are judged on what you can do. If you can play, you will play. If you can't play, you won't play.

An athlete, like everybody else, has to live with himself. He is called upon to do many things others aren't. He talks to newspapermen. He is interviewed on radio and television, reaching millions of listeners and touching their lives. It is not his duty to comment on things outside of his game or to bum-rap somebody else in airing his personal feelings. It is important to be yourself, be a man, accept things as a man.

As black athletes, if we speak out on various issues or wear our hair certain ways, we are considered militant, in opposition to The Establishment, which puts us in a position of being opposed to what gives us our livelihood. If we don't speak up about racial issues, political matters or the organization itself, we are called Uncle Toms.

There is a lot of talk about a shortage of representation for black athletes. It is my opinion that when you are involved in a team sport, you work as part of a team. Baseball is a special world. Our dreams are victories, home runs, no-hit games, pennants, winning the World Series, the All-Star game, being successful and enjoying the fun of playing the sport.

I don't regard it as a player's privilege to become involved in a lot of off-field issues or debates with management. Such men as Phil Wrigley, Horace Stoneham, Calvin Griffith and Tom Yawkey own their teams and make the best moves they can.

As for black versus white, it is my hope and dream that someday men will have more love and understanding for each other. The color of your skin, the cut of your clothes, the type of automobile you drive will have absolutely nothing to do with your acceptance by, or your respect for, your fellow man.

Blacks had a long uphill battle to break the color line in sports, especially in baseball. During the pre-Robinson days countless outstanding black players never had an opportunity to play in the major or minor leagues. Now things have changed. Besides black players, there are black coaches, scouts, umpires and administrators. Today's players must make certain that baseball will continue to welcome young blacks.

Johnny Sample wrote a book in which he criticized Buddy Young, an outstanding black football player at the University of Illinois who later played professional football for the Baltimore Colts. Buddy Young is a class gentleman. He has worked hard all his life and was respected by both his own teammates and opposing players in the collegiate and professional ranks. When he retired from playing, Buddy moved into the commissioner's office in professional football. Now he has duties and responsibilities important to the future of football. He cannot become involved in color or personal differences. As a good executive, Buddy has to make his decisions on the basis of ability and productivity. This doesn't make him an Uncle Tom.

I think we all must realize that the best job is done by the person who works hard at what he's doing. I would like to see my people spend more time applauding the progress of the Buddy Youngs and the Monte Irvins in the executive end of professional sports, giving them credit because they are going to help instead of hinder other blacks.

Not everyone will agree with me—and I consider this their privilege—but I've always said the only race we have in baseball is the run to beat the throw.

6

The College of Coaches

Near the end of spring training in 1954 the Cubs stopped in Dallas to play two exhibition games, giving me a chance to see my parents and family.

I arrived at the ball park the morning of the second day to find the clubhouse silent as a morgue, with manager Phil Cavarretta walking around aimlessly, mumbling to himself.

I whispered to Gene Baker, "What's wrong?"

"Cavarretta has been fired," Gene whispered back.

I figured Gene was pulling my leg. Making a second attempt to find out what was going on, I whispered, "Who's the new manager?"

Gene answered, "I don't know," still wearing a straight face. "Nothing has been said. Maybe they'll make you the new boss."

I had to rush to the toilet to make sure nobody saw me laughing.

The silence lasted until Cavarretta called the group to order and announced that he was being replaced. Phil thanked everyone for their cooperation and wished the Cubs, collectively and individually, good luck in the future, and then he walked out of the clubhouse. We all looked at each other, astonished.

"Fired during spring training. It just doesn't happen!"

During the pregame drills we gathered in groups trying to figure out what had happened. We were going to Shreveport, Louisiana, that evening, and by the time we got downtown to Dallas' Union Station the news was in the headlines:

Cavarretta Out, Hack In As Cubs' Manager

Ralph Kiner drew the day's first laugh when he said, "I'm going to ask Stan to change our goddamn signs before he does anything else. Everybody in the league has them now, especially the take sign. I've never seen so many fat pitches when the take sign is on. I swear I could hit 'em into the next county if I wasn't handcuffed to that damn sign."

There was a real difference between Cavarretta and Hack. Cavvy was an aggressive driver. When somebody was hurt, he would tell the trainer, "Tape him up and get him back out there so he can play." Hack was the happy type, always smiling, always the first to slap a player on the back after he had made a good play.

I had a good book on Stan before I met him. Gene Baker had played for Stan in Los Angeles, and during the train ride to Shreveport he told me about his regard for Hack.

I had played just ten games—at the end of the 1953 season—for Cavarretta, but I had found him a very good baseball man. During the previous winter Phil had invited me out to his home in Dallas and given me a few helpful hitting hints, revealing some of the plans he had for the Cubs and for me. When I left, I had felt good about finding a new friend. My visit to his home was especially significant because in Dallas a Negro didn't often make a social visit to a white man's home.

After his first clubhouse meeting with the players, Hack called me aside and said, "I had a visit with Bob Scheffing [one of the Cubs' coaches under Stan as well as Phil], and he suggested that we bat you third, ahead of Ralph Kiner and Hank Sauer. I think it's a good idea, and I just wanted you to know that's what we're planning to do. We're trying to get you an extra time at bat whenever possible."

During spring training I had alternated at shortstop with Roy Smalley, but he had logged more playing time because I had missed a week after being hit in the head by a pitch in an intra-squad game. Part of that time was spent in the hospital. Luckily, I recovered quickly.

The day we broke camp in Mesa, Arizona, I was

given an engraved wristwatch as the Cubs' No. 1 rookie of the spring. I guess I had finally become a real major leaguer.

We didn't set the National League afire during the 1954 season. We won sixty-four games, one less than the 1953 club, and again finished seventh. That was the year the Giants won a second pennant under Leo Durocher and swept the Cleveland Indians in the World Series.

On a beautiful day in Brooklyn in May 1955 Gene and I were hoofing it along Bedford Avenue to the subway. We had played an afternoon game at Ebbets Field and were headed for our room at the Commodore Hotel in Manhattan. Our dispositions, I'm sorry to say, didn't come close to matching the bright sunshine and warm weather. We hardly talked. We had just lost to the Dodgers.

We had walked only a few short blocks when a big Cadillac pulled to the curb and we heard a warm, friendly command: "Hop in."

Roy Campanella was at the wheel. Somehow he had spotted the two young Cubs' players in their civvies and had stopped to give us a ride.

We both knew Campy, and he had something more on his mind than just offering us a welcome ride. The late afternoon rush-hour traffic was heavy in both Brooklyn and New York, but Campy insisted on driving us right to the door of the Commodore.

On the way, he related his experiences as a rookie with the Dodgers, and he talked to us about some of the dos and don'ts for rookies coming into the majors. It wasn't a lecture, just an expression of his sincere interest in our success.

I don't remember hearing anybody express himself better than Campy did that day. He stressed the opportunities baseball had given him as well as us and the responsibility we all owed to the game in return.

"Just remember this, fellows," he said as we climbed out of the Caddy. "And at your age it's easy to forget: The higher you climb in baseball, the greater your responsibility will be all up and down the line, both on and off the field."

No one in baseball has earned more respect than Campy. I know this is true as I talk to younger players, such as Joe Morgan, Jimmy Wynn and Leron Lee. They don't know Campy, but they respect him for his achievements. I rate him with such people as Bill Blair and Buck O'Neil, whose help and leadership have been so important to my career.

After the Dodgers had won the pennant and defeated the New York Yankees in the 1955 World Series behind Johnny Podres' sensational pitching, we started out on a cross-country barnstorming junket. Eighteen or twenty major leaguers opposed a selected All-Star team from the Kansas City Monarchs and the Indianapolis Clowns. It was a fun-filled trip—and profitable since the major leaguers split up the big end of the gate in individual shares after each game.

When we got to Los Angeles, Gene was called home because of an accident involving his family. It was a tough break. Gene was a drawing card in Los Angeles, having played there for the Angels in the Pacific Coast League, and we would miss him since he had a good book on every blade of grass in the field.

Just before the game Don Newcombe sounded off, protesting the fact that our squad had voted Baker his full share of that day's gate. "He isn't here, and he doesn't deserve a red cent," Don argued.

The debate got so hot that Hank Thompson, who was on Baker's side, challenged Big Newk right then and there. It was tense, to say the least.

Then, in his own quiet but firm manner, Campy spoke up. "Don, what's the matter with you? The Dodgers won the pennant, and pretty soon you'll be getting a check for a winner's share of the World Series. It could amount to close to $10,000. This game's gate won't be much more than pin money compared to what you have coming.

"Of course we're going to give Baker his equal share. It isn't his fault that he isn't here. This isn't a factory where you punch a time clock. It's baseball."

Every player in the clubhouse applauded—even Newcombe. Gene was paid his full share. It was a good payday, too. That $750 was $350 more than I got for a whole thirty-day barnstorming trip in 1950.

Nobody knew better than I the importance of that money to Gene. We had just finished our second season with the Cubs, and we weren't receiving a winner's share of the World Series. I'm sure Campy realized this, too, when he spoke out on Baker's behalf.

Stan Hack remained our manager for one more year, 1956, but we just couldn't seem to win for him. We got up to sixth place in 1955 but fell into the cellar in 1956.

I finally found a way to get my name in the record book during 1955. Five of my forty-four homers that season were grand slams that set a major-league record for 154 games.

Records and the stories behind them are the talk of sports. I've been lucky enough to set a few records, but I had a hard time recovering from one of my early ones. I played my first game for the Chicago Cubs on September 17, 1953. Between then and August 10, 1956, when a finger infection forced me to the sidelines, I played 424 consecutive games. It was the longest string of games ever played by a rookie after breaking into a major-league lineup.

I missed a total of fifteen games because of the bad finger, and the inactivity while waiting for the injury to heal seemed like hell on earth. The Cubs weren't having a very good season, and there I was out of action, unable to make any kind of contribution. It was one of the few periods in my life when I got really discouraged.

After I returned to the lineup, I played another long string—717 games—which ended in Milwaukee on June 23, 1961. Then a knee injury forced me out of the lineup again.

Bob Scheffing, who won the 1956 Pacific Coast League championship by sixteen games with the Cubs' cousins, the Angels, became our manager for the 1957 season. John Holland, the general manager of the champion Angels, was moved to Chicago with Scheffing as an entry; and Scheffing, who had coached for both Cavarretta and Hack, imported two new coaches, Fred Fitzsimmons and George Myatt.

Fitzsimmons and Myatt concentrated on young pitchers, Bob Anderson, Johnny Briggs, Dick Drott, Glen Hobbie and Moe Drabowsky, a 1956 bonus signee out of Trinity College in Connecticut. Other newcomers were Cal Neeman, Frank Ernaga (who hit a home run his first time at bat in the majors), Bobby Morgan and Chuck Tanner (named the new manager of the Chicago White Sox during the closing weeks of the 1970 season).

On May 1, I lost my best friend and roommate, Gene Baker, in a deal with the Pittsburgh Pirates. Gene and Dee Fondy were traded to the Pirates for Dale Long and Lee Walls.

During Scheffing's first season we tied for seventh, but in 1958 and 1959 we moved up to fifth-place ties. These are two seasons I can remember very vividly. They were my Most Valuable Player years.

I was waiting to go to a Boys Club football banquet in November 1958 when I received a telephone call from Boston. The caller introduced himself as Hy Hurwitz, a sportswriter who was the secretary of the Baseball Writers' Association of America.

"We just finished counting a stack of ballots, and I have some good news for you," Hurwitz said. "You have just been elected the National League's Most Valuable Player. You are the fourth Cubs' player in history to win the award, and I want to congratulate you."

All I could say was, "Thank you very much. That is certainly good news."

He then told me Gabby Hartnett, Phil Cavarretta and Hank Sauer had been the Cubs' other MVP's.

It was about the same time a year later when Hurwitz called again to tell me I had won the MVP award a second time. "This is becoming a habit with you," Hurwitz said. I told him it was a very welcome habit and he could always call collect with that kind of news.

My glove, I'm sure, was as important as my bat in winning the second MVP award. In 1959 I had been lucky enough to set two major-league fielding records at shortstop: .985 for the highest percentage and only twelve errors in 155 games.

That year Dave Grote, the director of the National League service bureau, told me my total of 519 assists in one year outnumbered the assists Honus Wagner ever had in a year. You can be sure I never thought my name would be linked with the immortal Wagner's.

It has been my good fortune to have exceptional rapport with all my managers, but Bob Scheffing paid me the most flattering compliment I've ever received. In an interview, Scheffing said:

"During my first 26 years in baseball, Joe DiMaggio is the only player I'd ever consider rating ahead of Ernie Banks after the year Ernie had for me in 1959. He batted fourth behind three hitters who didn't come even close to averaging .260 and still he batted in 143 runs. He also hit 45 homers, and I figured out that his bat was directly responsible for 27 of our 74 victories that season. Afield he was the equal of any shortstop I've seen."

Starting in 1960 Charley Grimm became my fourth manager, and before the season ended I had a fifth boss: Lou Boudreau. Lou was the lone Cubs' import in the group. By this time people within the organization were planning the College of Coaches. It started in 1961.

Don Cardwell posted the Cubs' outstanding achievement in 1960 when he pitched a no-hit, no-run game against the St. Louis Cardinals for a 4–0 victory on May 15. This was only two days after we got him from the Philadelphia Phillies in a trade with Ed Bouchee for Tony Taylor and Cal Neeman.

Vedie Himsl was our head coach in 1961 when the Cubs called a noontime press conference on May 23 to announce two moves: the installation of Jerry Kindall at shortstop and the transfer of Ernie Banks to left field. Kindall had been a key player when the University of Minnesota won the Big Ten and the NCAA baseball championships under Dick Siebert, a longtime major leaguer. Jerry was younger and faster than I was, with good range and an outstanding glove. He had been a bonus signee with the Cubs when he graduated from college in 1956.

When reporters asked me about the move, I told them straight out that the knee I had injured during

Clockwise from right: Ernie in 1954; hit in St. Louis— Banks' 44th homer of the 1955 season was also his fifth grand slam that year; Banks to Baker for the double play (Eddie Mathews sliding).

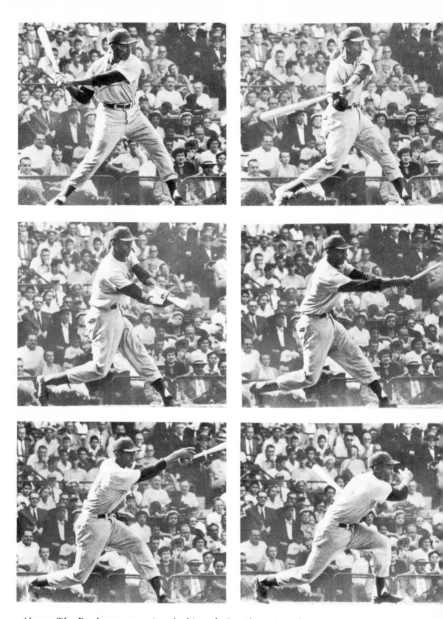

Above: The Banks power swing, fashioned after the swing of Hank Thompson during softball days. Top right: Ben Banks, Ernie's brother, signs a Cub contract. Bottom right: Chicago baseball writers honor Ernie, Warren Giles and Tommy Byrne.

Top: Ernie hitting, in 1958.
Umpire is Frank Dascoli. Above:
Ernie lights dad's cigar on
Father's Day. Two cigars
meant the game was a close one.

Left: Ernie makes room on his mantel for latest trophy—1958 Most Valuable Player. Below: After winning fielding crown in 1959, Ernie is invited to New York to give lessons to kids.

Clockwise from right: Back safely to first under tag of Mets' Gil Hodges; Ernie receives two awards at Chicago's Diamond Dinner— presenting the awards is the author; meanwhile, back at the mantel, wife Eloyce shows off 1959 MVP trophy; Cubs' owner Phil Wrigley examines Ernie's stat sheet after ordering rest for Ernie's knee and bad eye.

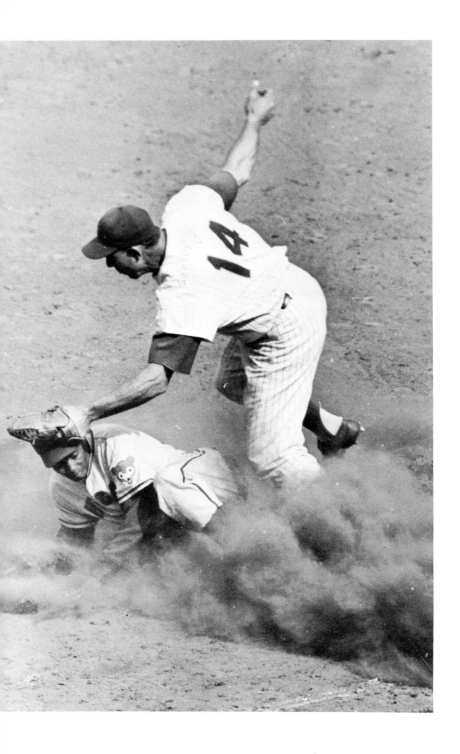

*Clockwise from right:
Batting practice in
Mesa, Arizona, 1962;
Ernie and Buck O'Neil
are reunited in 1962
when Buck is made a
Cub coach. O'Neil
managed the Monarchs
when Ernie played
there; Banks tagged
out by Dodger catcher
John Roseboro; in
1962 game against
the Reds, Ernie is
hit in back of neck
by Moe Drabowsky.*

Clockwise from right: Ernie, dad, wife, sons on Ernie Banks Day; signing autographs on his Day, the first such day in Cub history; giving his two sons and friend a hitting lesson.

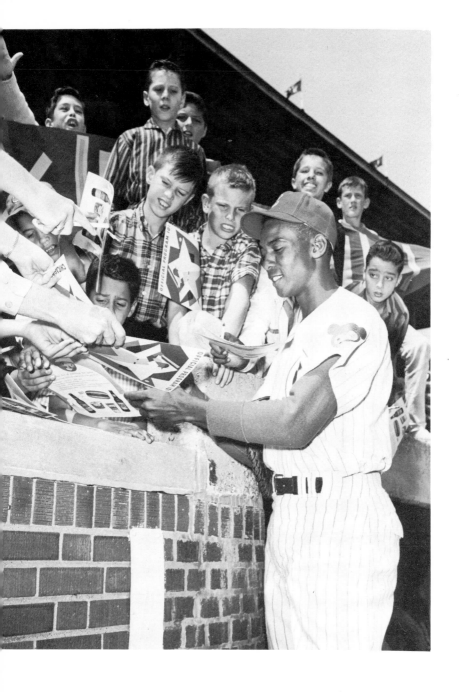

*Clockwise from left: Ernie reaches
for the plate after oversliding
while Phillies' catcher Dalrymple looks
for ball; Ernie scores his 1,000th
run as a Cub; George Altman, Satchel
Paige and Ernie Banks get together
during a pregame ceremony in Chicago.*

Clockwise from left: Ernie encourages kids to stay in school; teammate Ron Santo and Ernie spend some time with a young Chicago fan; Ernie and his wife meet with Pope Paul VI during trip to Rome.

Clockwise from right: Ernie makes his way from barracks to barracks during 1968 tour of forces in Saigon; while in Saigon, Ernie naturally gives time to the children; handshake with infantryman. In rear is pitcher Richert.

Eddie, Essie, Ernie.

Clockwise from above: Stan Musial listens to Ernie's 1968 "good-guy" award; Ernie waves to crowd after 2,500th hit; Ernie wears button in attempt to win the 1969 NL pennant.

Left: "Mr. Cub" hits another homer. Above: Sons Joey (center) and Jerry admire their father's newest trophy—presented by the Wisconsin Baseball Writers to Ernie Banks in 1970 with title "Mr. Baseball."

*Above: Shaking hands with
the President during White
House reception before 1969
All-Star Game. Right: As
a member of the Chicago Transit
Authority, Ernie was asked
to model at special luncheon.*

Ernie Banks, in pictures on these two pages, is a wrist hitter, a batter who gets line drives as well as long balls.

Clockwise from below: Ernie shows ball he hit for 500th homer to family, including daughter Jan Elizabeth; happiness is 500 homers; the swing that got $500, May 12, 1970, at Wrigley Field, vs. Braves.

Ernie Banks, "Mr. Cub."

spring training was giving me some pain—especially when I made quick lateral moves.

Only a duck out of water could have shared my loneliness in left field. I had never played the outfield, and the first thing I thought about was all the tricky wind currents Hank Sauer, Ralph Kiner and Moose Moryn had talked about when they played left field for the Cubs. Fortunately, Richie Ashburn, the Cubs' center fielder, became a real friend during my twenty-three-game outfield career.

"Just listen for my call, I'll try to guide you on everything hit to left-center," Richie volunteered, and he didn't let me down. He deserves credit for at least 50 percent of my thirty-two put-outs and six assists as a left fielder. How I managed to escape with just one error in twenty-three games will always be a mystery.

In mid-June when the Cubs were playing in San Francisco, Elvin Tappe, then our head coach, asked me to join him for breakfast. Somewhere between the orange juice and the ham and eggs Tappe asked me what my reaction would be to moving to first base. Had he asked me to catch I would have done it—anything to get out of left field.

I told Tappe something I'm sure he knew—that I would do anything to help the Cubs. He replied that there had been some top level discussions among the coaches, and they would like to try the move. Charley Grimm would help me with my first-base play during the pregame drills that night.

I had a tutor, but what I didn't have was a first

baseman's mitt. When we got to the park, André Rodgers loaned me one of his for the workout and for my first game as a first baseman.

During his playing days Charley Grimm had been a great fielding first baseman and a magician with the mitt. Like a student cramming for an examination, I asked him every question I could think of during that drill, but there was an important difference between professor and pupil: Grimm was left-handed; I was right-handed.

At the start of the game I had three things going for me: Grimm's tips, Rodgers' glove and my relief at getting out of left field.

During the Giants' half of the first inning, Joe Amalfitano (who later played for the Chicago Cubs before becoming a Cubs' coach) hit a grounder to Don Zimmer, our second baseman. I ran to cover first and positioned both my feet on the bag. Amalfitano was coming hard down the line—right at me.

At the last second Joe swerved to his right to avoid hitting me, a stationary first baseman still standing on the base. Running as hard as he was, Joe spared us both possible serious injuries when he swerved instead of plowing straight across the bag. Since then I've thanked him many times—and I learned an important lesson that day: never stand on the base to catch a throw. Amalfitano's nickname is Pal Joey, and I subscribe to that 100 percent.

The Giants gave me a lot of ribbing during that game. "So you've finally made it to the old people's home in baseball," they said. "First base is the last stop before you hang 'em up." And Willie Mays, always a frustrated first baseman, kept yelling instructions to me about where to play, how to shift and when to break with the pitch.

When I was still a shortstop, I appeared on a television show in New York with Campy and Polly Bergen. In our skit Miss Bergen asked my name and what position I played. I told her my name was Ernie Banks and that I played shortstop for the Chicago Cubs. When she asked the location of my particular base, I told her the shortstop didn't have a base since he played between the second and third basemen. The skit ended with Miss Bergen saying, "My poor boy, playing without a base. Maybe someday, if you play long enough, you'll end up with a base you can call your very own."

There can be no question that my move to first base has prolonged my career and I've been happy playing there. It's not a bad place to call my own.

7

Keep the Faith

After the 1958 season I had a noontime meeting with a friend to discuss a business proposition. As I was getting off the elevator in a Wabash Avenue building in Chicago's Loop, I noticed an attractive receptionist in another office on the same floor. We exchanged smiles. When I left, we both waved and I said to myself, "I'll see *you* later!"

I'm not sure whether I was more interested in the business proposition or the receptionist when I went back the next day. After the second meeting, I walked over and introduced myself to the girl. Her name was Eloyce Johnson. She was a native of Tyler, Texas, and the firm she was working for specialized in public relations. At that time Sammy Davis, Jr., was the firm's big-name account.

I left after a short conversation, but I knew I'd be back, and I'm sure Miss Johnson knew this too. I was —the very next day. This time I asked her to dinner and a show. She accepted, saying theater tickets were no problem—the firm had a lot of entertainers as clients.

Several dates later Eloyce told me she was going to California to spend the holidays with her parents. Her father, Rasberry Johnson, had taught school in Texas for forty years before moving his family to Los Angeles. About that same time I was to be in Los Angeles for a sports award dinner.

The night after the banquet I invited Eloyce out for dinner and asked her to marry me. All she said was "When?" I said right now, and within a few minutes we were in a taxi bound for the Los Angeles airport to catch a plane to Las Vegas.

The following day we returned to Los Angeles to tell her parents we had eloped. They were surprised but happy. Mrs. Johnson, a twenty-five-year teacher in east Texas schools before her retirement, was a bit reserved at first and asked me what I did for a living. I was glad I had all the right answers.

After the holidays we returned to Chicago and decided to wait until spring training to take our honeymoon in Mesa, Arizona.

The following fall we were blessed with twin sons, Joey and Jerry. They were born in California because Eloyce had gone back to Los Angeles to be near her mother and sisters.

House hunting came next. We found a large house

at 8159 South Rhodes Avenue on Chicago's South Side and moved in immediately.

A few nights later, Eloyce woke me up sounding very upset.

"Something is wrong! Jerry is having trouble with his breathing."

We called the doctor. He said I should bundle up Jerry and meet him at St. Bernard's Hospital, where he was on the staff. I beat the doctor to the hospital and waited nervously for him to arrive. During the wait a friendly nun asked if Jerry had been baptized. In my condition I'm not sure what I said, but it really didn't matter. The nun started sprinkling. Jerry was sprinkled with holy water and duly baptized.

I had forgotten all about the incident until Jerry recovered and the doctor called to say, "Eloyce and Ernie, it could only happen to you. Do you know that your twins are very unusual? Jerry is a Catholic, and Joey is a Protestant!"

The nun, happy over Jerry's full recovery, had told the doctor how she had baptized our son the night he arrived at the hospital. The story has been a family joke since, and I've often wondered just how many sets of Catholic-Protestant twins there are. One thing's for sure. No one will ever be able to say my kids didn't "keep the faith."

We were able to get our new home furnished in time for the holidays, and this was the first Christmas I ever spent complete with all the trimmings: Santa

Claus, a tree and gifts for all the family, including Eloyce's parents and mine.

The twins were four years old when Jan Elizabeth, our daughter, was born.

Both of our sons play Little League baseball. Jerry is a second baseman, and Joey alternates between third base and left field. Both have a deep interest in sports and have been fortunate to meet Willie Mays, Lew Alcindor, Gale Sayers, Bobby Hull and most of my Cubs' teammates as well as some of the White Sox' players.

I've been able to take the twins on some trips with the Cubs, and in this way we get to do a lot of sight-seeing we've visited the historic sites in most of the National League cities. The twins were involved in one situation in Atlanta that I never will forget. After we won the first game, the twins came into the clubhouse and saw everybody talking happily and congratulating each other. The next night we lost, and when the twins came into the clubhouse everybody was quiet. Joey was so surprised, he asked me what was the matter right then and there.

I promised I would explain everything when we got back to the hotel. The incident provided the opportunity to explain to both boys that winning is happiness and losing is unhappiness. It's not the worst thing in the world to lose, but . . .

I've taken the twins and their sister to spring training several times since we have been able to enroll them in Arizona schools. Already they have done more horse-back riding than I ever did—and they love it.

Unless there is a sudden switch, I don't think there will be much "like father, like son" in our family. When Jerry talks about his favorite sport, it's basketball. Hockey for Joey. When I grew up in Dallas, I didn't even know there was a game called hockey!

Through the 1960 season I had a total of 269 homers, but I really didn't think I had a chance to reach .500. One spectacular day in 1962 I did much better. We were playing the Milwaukee Braves in Wrigley Field and I doubled the first time up against Bob Hendley. During my next three times at bat I hit successive home runs off three different pitchers—Hendley; Don Nottebart, a former Cubs' teammate, and Lew Burdette. We lost the game, 11–9.

After my third homer, Hank Aaron asked, "Who is the man in the control tower of your friendly windmill? Every time you come to the plate he turns it on, and the wind blows a gale toward the outfield fences."

In 1963 I thought my career was over. I had just returned to the lineup after missing a few games as the result of being hit in the head by a pitch. My hitting was off because of faulty vision, and the old knee injury slowed down my mobility. We were in St. Louis when I was told that Phil Wrigley wanted me to return to Chicago for tests. He had personally arranged for the best medical talent available, and ordered me to take some time out and relax. I missed twenty-five games.

I had played my fourth three-homer game on June

9 against the Dodgers in Wrigley Field. I got the first two homers off Sandy Koufax and the third off Larry Sherry. We had lost this game, 11–8, and I hit only five more home runs the rest of my unhappy season.

The Cubs had three shining knights in 1964. Larry Jackson won twenty-four games, the most by a Cubs' pitcher since Charlie Root captured twenty-six in 1927, and Ron Santo and Billy Williams became a great slugging twosome: 63 home runs and 212 runs-batted-in between them. Larry put together a nine-game winning streak before he lost his last decision of the year shooting for No. 25.

The Cubs finished eighth in 1965, but they had the only threesome of hitters in the league with more than 300 runs-batted-in among them: Williams (108), Banks (106) and Santo (101).

8

Concentration

During the early stages of my career I didn't regard myself as a home-run hitter—nor was I alone in my thinking. After Richie Ashburn came to the Cubs following his great years with the Phillies, he told me:

"Ernie, when you first came up to the majors, I figured you to be another Punch and Judy hitter and I'd play you accordingly. Whenever you'd come to the plate, I'd shift to short right-center. You were good for one or two outs every game because I never had to move more than a dozen steps one way or the other to catch the ball."

I might still be a "Punch and Judy hitter" if it hadn't been for certain timely advice from greats Hank Thompson, Ralph Kiner, Jackie Robinson and Monte Irvin.

Before I had even joined the Colts—during a soft-ball game in Dallas—Thompson taught me stance and the importance of a smooth, level swing. Robinson was the first to stress the need for more and more hitting practice, with emphasis on trying to pull the ball. From Kiner I learned the importance of bat selection and Irvin taught me how weather can affect the weight of the bat.

Early in my career Irvin came to Wrigley Field with the New York Giants for a series in mid-July. The blistering sun forced the temperature to well over 100 degrees on the field. During the pregame drills, Monte asked, "What's wrong, Ernie? You don't look like the same hitter you were just two weeks ago."

As we chatted back and forth he wanted to know if I was using the same bat during the hot spell that I had used earlier when the weather was cooler. I told him I was. He had the Giants' bat boy bring me a couple of his lighter models and they worked like a charm.

Irvin's gift bats weighed thirty-one ounces with a lighter and smaller handle. Before Monte gave me his bats I was using Babe Ruth's R43 model, which weighed thirty-three and a half ounces—and you can't believe what a big difference those two and a half ounces made during that particular hot spell.

Later in my career I switched to Vern Stephens' S2 model. It's a regular 36 (ounces)–35 (inches long). During the hot summer days my friend Frank Ryan, an executive of the Louisville Slugger bat company, had some thirty-two- and thirty-three-ounce models made up for me to use.

There is an ironic touch to my use of Vern Stephens' model. Vern set the major-league record I broke when he hit 39 home runs playing shortstop for the Boston Red Sox in 1949.

In baseball it's an age-old claim that "good hitters are born, not developed." I refuse to refute that, but I've found that practice and concentration help hitting. During a discussion about hitters and hitting, Hank Sauer once said:

"Ask a hundred different players for tips about hitting, and you will receive a hundred different versions of what is right and what is wrong."

There have been times when I thought concentration was more important than practice. Once, while locked in a slump, I met Dr. Morris Friedell, a physician on Chicago's South Side.

"I've been watching you on television, Ernie, and you just aren't concentrating," Dr. Friedell claimed. "You aren't even close to making contact with the ball. I've played enough golf to know concentration is the name of the game. I'm sure it's just as important in hitting."

We discussed the concentration subject at length, and the next day I was 3-for-3 before getting an intentional walk my last time at bat.

Concentration was a most important factor in two of my first nine career-grand-slam home runs: number five off Lindy McDaniel in 1955, and number nine off Stu Miller in 1961. I'd never had too much success hitting against either pitcher—and I realized the time had come to do something different.

McDaniel, then in his youth, had an exceptionally good sinking fast ball as well as a hard slider—the same pitch Larry Jackson later used so effectively in becoming a twenty-four game winner for the Cubs. I made up my mind in advance that I would attempt to hit under the very first low sinker McDaniel threw to me. I got it on the first pitch, and the ball carried into the left-field bleachers.

Miller was a successful off-speed pitcher because he had pinpoint control of his slow and slower breaking pitches. When he first came up they called Stu "the Eddie Lopat of the National League," and believe me he earned the compliment. Miller often moved his head as part of his delivery, and I know I was swinging at his head more than I ever did at his pitch.

This day I decided I would attempt to aim right at him in trying to hit the ball up the middle instead of pulling the pitch. I did, and the ball landed in the left side of the center-field bleachers in Wrigley Field.

Whenever I see Dr. Friedell, he always asks: "How are you doing with your concentration?" I wouldn't know if Dr. Friedell ever swung a bat, but I do know he was a tremendous help to me.

During my entire career I've always made it a point to watch and study the delivery of every pitcher when he warms up. You can see a pitcher five or six times during a season and still not learn everything about his delivery or his pitches. I do this because I regard baseball as war between the pitcher and the hitter. He's trying to make you hit his pitch, and you're determined to wait for your pitch.

Maturity generates better and deeper concentration, especially when applied to batting practice. During my career I've been helped considerably by men like Roy Johnson, Ray Blades, Buck O'Neil, Stan Hack, Bob Scheffing and Lou Boudreau. All of them would throw nothing but breaking pitches in batting practice, the better to prepare me for game conditions when I would see many more curve balls than fast balls.

All of these men had great theories about hitting that they shared with me—in discussions as well as at batting practice. During most of my meat-and-potato years first Hack and then Scheffing talked overtime to help make me conscious of seeing mainly breaking balls in situations where men are on base. Often Scheffing would say:

"Get ready for the curve ball. That's all you're going to see, because no pitcher is going to let you hurt him with a fast ball in a tight spot."

Although he was my manager for only a part of one season, I've spent enough time with Boudreau to learn most of his scientific hints on hitting.

During recent seasons, after he came to the Cubs from the San Francisco Giants, Randy Hundley has spent a lot of time talking both baseball and hitting with me. Randy is very knowledgeable. His theories are among the best I've ever heard. His book on the hitters in the National League has added to his value to the Cubs.

Johnny Logan of the Milwaukee Braves was an outstanding breaking-ball hitter and his success was the result of overtime practice. Whenever Logan was in the cage during batting practice, all you ever heard him say to the pitcher was "curve ball," a command that preceded every pitch. Ted Williams, Stan Musial and Hank Aaron were or are tremendous curve-ball hitters for the very same reason. They always called for more curves than fast balls. Aaron still does.

During a four-year span in the late 50s I had a total of 176 home runs and 491 runs-batted-in. These are totals one hitter can't obtain alone. He has to have help, and I had a lot of it. Lee Walls batted third, just ahead of me, and had a .287 average for three of these four years.

Moose Moryn was the Cubs' fifth-place hitter, and he had a four-season total of 72 home runs. The potency of the Walls and Moryn bats, I'm sure, had a lot to do with me getting pitches I might not have seen otherwise.

Sam Jones proved concentration is as important to pitching as it is to hitting when he threw the first major-league no-hit, no-run game I ever played in. It was against Pittsburgh, and Sam walked the bases full to start the ninth. We had a 4–0 lead at the time, and whenever I looked into the dugout I could see manager Stan Hack inching closer to the steps. Finally he was standing on the top step when Sam walked the third Pirate to fill the bases.

All the infielders were yelling encouragement to Sam, who reacted as if he didn't hear a single thing we were saying. He just continued to chew on his ever-present toothpick. Outside an occasional look to check the outfielders' positions, big Sam kept his eyes trained on home plate in complete silence. What followed was one of the most outstanding pitching performances I've ever seen.

Jones fanned Dick Groat on three pitches. Roberto Clemente fouled off two pitches before he struck out. Now Sam was just one out away, but he appeared to be throwing harder to Frank Thomas than he had to either Groat or Clemente. His fourth pitch to Thomas was a called third strike. Three walks and three strike-outs in one inning to save a no-hitter.

While we listened to part of the replay on the radio in the clubhouse afterward, we learned it was a really historic game—the first no-hit, no-run game in Wrigley Field in 37 years. Later Sam told us:

"When I realized I was on the verge of blowing one of the better games I ever pitched, I told myself: 'They aren't going to get a hit now.' I heard you fellows yelling at me, but I was determined not to let anything bother my concentration. I was going to get those last three outs . . . and that's all I thought about."

I say Sam left nothing to chance, fanning three solid hitters like Groat, Clemente and Thomas on just 12 pitches. That's concentration in full bloom.

9

Life with Leo

In 1966, after the five-year reign of the College of Coaches, the Cubs imported another manager—Leo Durocher. The timing was perfect. Leo was the man most of the fans and the people in baseball were talking about as he returned to the job he liked and knew best: managing. Because of Durocher's signing, the off-season of the fall of 1965 and the spring of 1966 was the busiest in modern Cubs' history.

Eddie Stanky had also returned to the game; he had signed to manage the White Sox. So Leo and Eddie, the manager-player combination from the New York Giants' miracle pennant-winning team of 1951, were back in business. The two of them did a lot of kidding in the news media. Once when Stanky's name was mentioned, Leo told a sports gathering, "I've already told Eddie—

the South Side is his, and this is fine with me. The North Side belongs to me and me alone. If he dares put one foot north of Madison Street [the south-north boundary line in Chicago], I'll have him tossed in the river wearing a concrete kimono."

During January the Cubs arranged a first-of-its-kind winter press caravan through Wisconsin, Iowa, Illinois and Indiana, featuring Leo and a half-dozen players. Leo was the star, and he talked overtime, saying:

"The Cubs aren't an eighth-place club, and I'm here to find out why they are where they are."

"If I can't win with one team, I'll back up the truck and get me another, because I refuse to stand still."

"If, after winning a game, one of my players wants a night on the town, all he has to do is call me up—I'll go along with him."

Interest in the Cubs perked up immediately. The fans looked to the future with new hope.

In 1966 we trained in Long Beach, California, and Leo lost little time letting us know where we stood—and why. The New Order was Durocher's Order, from start to finish.

We lost eight of our first nine games in 1966 and finished tenth behind the two expansion clubs, the Houston Astros and the New York Mets. We had lost more than a hundred games but there was Leo's fine hand planning and plotting for the future with younger players.

Larry Jackson and Bob Buhl were traded early to Philadelphia for Ferguson Jenkins, Adolfo Phillips and Johnny Herrnstein. Ken Holtzman became our only pitcher to win more than eight games, an impressive record for a twenty-year-old who was pitching for a 103-game losing team.

From tenth in 1966, the Cubs climbed to a surprising third-place finish in 1967. It was the first time the Cubs had finished in the first division since 1946. Leo's patience and handling of young players, such as Holtzman, Glenn Beckert, Don Kessinger and Randy Hundley, had paid quick returns. We won twenty-eight more games in 1967 than we did in 1966 and fourteen out of fifteen games in one streak. The Cubs' future was getting brighter.

It was during this season—July 2 to be exact—that I enjoyed my greatest day as a Cub, without even playing. The previous day I had been sidelined with a spiked heel, the result of an unavoidable collision with Pete Rose of the Cincinnati Reds at first base. Now, as I watched from the WGN radio booth in Wrigley Field with Vince Lloyd and Lou Boudreau, I saw Ferguson Jenkins beat the Reds and Sammy Ellis, 4–1. This victory and the St. Louis Cardinals' loss of the first game of a doubleheader to the Mets in New York gave the Cubs undisputed possession of first place.

More than thirty-seven thousand fans helped root the Cubs to victory, and at least half the fans remained in the park to follow the progress of the Cardinals' second game on the scoreboard as the score was posted every half inning. St. Louis won to pull back into a tie, but our fans still danced with joy, and so did I.

The Cubs tied for first place two more times, July 22 and 24, but our luck ran out after that.

Ferguson Jenkins had a twenty-game winning season that year, and Ken Holtzman, using weekend passes from his military drills during the second half of the season, won nine straight games without a loss. Ken achieved this flawless record pitching only ninety-three innings in twelve games. Think what his record might have been had he been available for the entire season!

We finished third again in 1968, sandwiched between the second-place San Francisco Giants and the Cincinnati Reds. Now almost everybody agreed that the Cubs had arrived—under Leo's leadership.

Jenkins repeated his twenty-game winning mark in 1968, but this statistic doesn't tell the entire story for the big Canadian. Five of his fifteen defeats were 1–0 losses to equal a major-league record—not completely to Fergie's liking.

After the 1968 season, the National League expanded to twelve teams by adding Montreal and San Diego. The Cubs were entered in the Eastern Division with the St. Louis Cardinals, Pittsburgh Pirates, Philadelphia Phillies, New York Mets and Montreal Expos.

In the preseason polls we were picked as the Cardinals' biggest rivals for the 1969 Eastern Division championship. We opened with an extra-inning victory over the Phillies and led our division for 156 consecutive days. Cubs' fans everywhere had visions of our first flag since 1945 and Chicago's first World Series since 1959, when the White Sox had won the American League pennant.

Moving into September, we had a three-and-a-half-game lead with twenty-two games to play. It looked as if we would go all the way.

Who knows what happened then? Something did. We went into a slump and just couldn't recover. Everything we had been doing right for five months we now did wrong. The fielding, the hitting and the pitching all went sour together. We just couldn't win for losing.

It was September 10—a date I'll never forget—when we lost in Philadelphia and the Mets beat Montreal in New York. The Mets moved into the lead, dropping us into second place. We never regained the lead as the Mets moved on to the divisional title and then swept the Atlanta Braves for the National League championship, finally capping it all by winning the World Series from the Baltimore Orioles.

Everybody asks: "What happened?"

Many, almost too many, explanations have been offered for our sad September. Some said our decline was the result of too much commercialism as the players became involved in outside interests. I doubt that very much.

Others reasoned that our failure could be traced to two things: the Cubs' complete lack of experience under pennant pressure and fatigue. Phil Regan, our outstanding relief pitcher, was the only Cubs' player who had ever been through the wringer before. He had pitched for the Los Angeles Dodgers when they won the pennant in 1966.

The fatigue, they said, was the result of playing a set lineup game after game. I remember one World Series discussion in New York that compared the Cubs' failure with an all-night poker game. As long as you are winning, you never give it a thought. Then you begin losing and your nerves fray. Your spirits fall and playing just isn't the thing anymore. When we were winning, the team's spirits were high. When we were losing, we would sit around the clubhouse staring into space, puzzled over our fate.

The one thing we all realized was that no one player was to blame. We had skidded into this slump together and absolutely nothing we tried could pull us back on top.

It wasn't until mid-November that Leo finally talked about the Cubs' failure. Speaking to a group of transportation executives in Chicago, he said, "I could have dressed nine broads up as ballplayers, and they would have beaten the Cubs. No lie.

"I never saw anything like it in my life. Our offense went down the toilet, the defense went down the drain, and I'm still looking for our pitching staff.

"Oh, we were bad, so bad. Lousy is the word for it. Just plain lousy, period."

This was rough reading, especially when the words came from the manager after such a tough September. But the following February when we assembled for spring training, the Cubs were once again one big happy family. Leo had joked. Never again did we hear anything about the nine broads. But that's Leo all the way —a bark now, a good laugh a little later. He does it to keep us on our toes. When we see Leo laugh, we forget about what may have happened to us in the past and think only about the winning future.

On the other hand, Leo can build a player's morale like no one else. After the Cubs lost in 1966, there was considerable speculation about what would happen to old man Ernie Banks. There was talk that John Boccabella, a collegian from Santa Clara, or Clarence Jones from the Cubs' farm system would be my successor at first base. The Cubs were rebuilding with youth, and I could understand the situation. Nonetheless, I refused to let anything dampen my desire to keep right on playing.

When I was given a new player-coach contract on February 28, 1967—shortly after the Cubs opened their new spring camp in Scottsdale, Arizona—my determination to have a good year for the Chicago Cubs just doubled.

The Cubs gave me my first two-year contract for the 1968 and 1969 seasons. After our third-place finish in 1967, Leo had said, "I don't know where Ernie keeps getting those pep pills, but I've got to check out his favorite pharmaceutical house and get a double order for myself." I was grateful.

I can speak with tremendous professional pride about 1969—that year I was lucky enough to lead National League first basemen with a fielding percentage of .997 hitched to a league-leading total of 1,419 putouts. That's four errors out of 1,510 chances.

Speaking about first base, I've now played 1,283 games there. That's 226 more than I played at short. I've played 2,489 games, including 57 at third and 23 in left field, and 69 as a pinch hitter. My next goal in the majors is to reach the 2,500 game mark. That and 500 home runs are two totals any player would like to have listed with his career record.

Leo is unlike any other manager I've ever played for. His one-word motto is WIN. He won a pennant with the Dodgers in Brooklyn and two with the New York Giants. I'm just as sure that he will help the Chicago Cubs win their next pennant. He detests association with a loser.

Many times I've been asked if I wanted to answer Leo's command to the sportswriters to quit calling me "Mr. Cub." My answer always has been—and always will be—no. I've never felt it was within my prerogative to tell writers what to write or what not to write.

Leo's talk to the players before our last game in 1969—long before he spoke out about the nine broads —was one of the finest I've heard. He was, right then, as brokenhearted over the Cubs' failure to win the Eastern Division championship as all the rest of us. He spoke like a champion to make us feel like champions, even though we finished second.

Whenever Durocher first reaches the ball park, he is calm and relaxed. He will kid or play cards with his players after meeting with the coaches to discuss game plans. Later, especially when the Cubs are playing in Wrigley Field, he stops in the bullpen to check the warm-up of his starting pitcher. Then he moves into the dugout where he becomes more aware and edgy. Leo likes a lot of runs early in the game. They give him freedom to maneuver.

Defensively, Leo works mainly with his center fielder and catcher. He will move the center fielder right or left, shallow or deep, depending on who is at bat. He directs most of his catchers pretty closely, expecting them to look into the dugout often to check pitching signals.

Leo's main strategy is getting a big lead early in the game. Whenever Bob Gibson or Juan Marichal is pitching, Leo wants his hitters to wait them out—by not swinging at too many first pitches, he forces them to throw the ball over the plate.

Dugout tension really grows whenever a hitter takes a called third strike with runners on base. Leo never eases off during a game; he cannot be comfortable, even with a big lead.

When he goes to the bullpen telephone, he wants immediate action. He likes his relief pitchers to pop up and start throwing quickly. Leo's decisions are quick and a player's reaction to them has to be just as rapid. If he wants you to pinch-hit, you grab a bat and a helmet and hit. If a player is in the dugout runway and misses his first command, Leo will say "Forget it!" and order another man to go in instead.

Leo compliments everyone who does an exceptional job. Because he is an attack-minded manager, his greatest pleasure seems to come from watching a pinch hitter who gets the game-winning hit.

Leo generally sticks with a set lineup and while he never says it, you can feel the confidence he has in certain players.

Durocher usually has words for the opposing team. Whenever Bob Gibson is pitching against the Cubs, he yells to the umpires, "Make him slow down out there."

He tells his players, "You guys know Gibson likes to work fast. Step out of the box and make him wait or slow down. Stall him!"

The Atlanta Braves' Ron Reed is a big, slow workman, who often lets the count go to three and two. Reed bothers Durocher as much as Gibson, and Leo will often yell impatiently, "Come on, Alice, let's go out there."

Leo is like three different people on game day. Before the game he is calm, relaxed and happy. During the game he is as tense as a general directing his troops. Afterward, if we win, he reverts to his pregame attitude. If we lose, and it is a routine loss, he is quiet. If it is a game he thought we lost on a bad play, he really lets us have it.

In 1970 when we beat out the New York Mets for

second place in the Eastern Division in the last game of the year, we detected a slight change in Durocher's post-game attitude.

"OK, gang, you gave it a good try!" he said.

10

The Wrigley Method

People often ask me if I've ever had any regrets over the selling of my contract by the Kansas City Monarchs to the Chicago Cubs instead of to one of the longtime winning clubs, such as the Yankees or the Dodgers. The answer is no, loud and clear.

I figure that Ernie Banks is the luckiest person in the world to be associated with the very best organization in baseball—the Chicago Cubs.

What makes the Cubs so outstanding? A man named Mr. Phil Wrigley, who gives his time and knowledge unselfishly to the good of baseball. He is kind, considerate, helpful, understanding and loyal, and Wrigley never thinks of the Cubs alone. It's baseball, and then the Cubs.

Mr. Wrigley, his son William and John Holland,

the Cubs' vice president, aren't just employers, they are friends. I have never considered an investment or a business venture without discussing it first with Mr. Wrigley. His door is always open. If he likes the idea, he'll say so. If he doesn't like it, he'll also say so, and why.

I'm not known for my low boiling point, but any time Mr. Wrigley is criticized about anything concerning baseball, I blow. I automatically figure the writer or the commentator has his facts mixed up.

Probably the man with the best book on Wrigley is Jimmy Gallagher, a former general manager and Cubs' vice president. Mr. Gallagher has told me how Phil Wrigley helped pioneer Chicago baseball on radio and later on television and how the Cubs' operation is always looking for ways to improve the fans' comfort in Wrigley Field.

I'm told the Cubs' handling of tickets for the seventh game of the 1945 World Series against the Detroit Tigers was a Wrigley innovation, one typical of his outlook. When it became obvious there would be a seventh game, Mr. Wrigley and his staff tried to get in touch with every fan whose original request for tickets had been turned down for lack of space. Each one was offered tickets for this last game.

Naturally, 99 percent of the fans who had been disappointed earlier jumped at the opportunity to see the deciding game, and I've been told that the 41,590 in attendance represented more rank-and-file fans than in any other game in World Series' history.

I've also been told that Mr. Wrigley, as owner of the Cubs, personally could have blocked the Braves' move from Boston to Milwaukee in 1952 with a "no" vote since Milwaukee is within a hundred-mile radius of Chicago. Instead, he sent his representatives to the National League owners' meeting in Florida with instructions to vote "yes" if the Braves requested the transfer. When asked why he bypassed an opportunity to head off more direct competition for the Cubs, Mr. Wrigley answered, "If Lou Perini thinks he can operate more successfully in Milwaukee than Boston, I must respect his thinking. After all, he does own the team and should be allowed to operate it as he sees fit."

I know from personal experience that Wrigley's timing usually is as good as his judgment. After my poor season in 1963, I went to the Mayo Clinic in Rochester, Minnesota, for a complete physical examination. They gave me every possible test, and then sent me back to Chicago with a clean bill of health. After landing in Chicago, I went to Wrigley Field to give Mr. Holland a full report on the good news. Holland suggested that we go downtown and report the Mayo findings in person to Mr. Wrigley.

We talked to Mr. Wrigley for about an hour, and when I finally got up to leave, he placed a piece of paper in my hand. I didn't have to look hard to see it was a baseball contract; my contract for 1964 with the same salary I had received in 1963.

Naturally I was surprised. When I asked if there wasn't some mistake, Mr. Wrigley said, "Ernie, that is the way we planned it. We have full confidence that you will bounce back and have a good year in 1964. The doctors have given you good news, and we are merely trying to keep pace, providing you with more good news." Whenever Mr. Wrigley speaks, he uses "we" instead of "I."

I've got to think I'm one of the very few players ever to suffer a 42 percentage point skid in his batting average—.269 in 1962 to .227 in 1963—and still play for the same pay a year later.

During the 1961 season when an eye problem and the troublesome knee injury forced me to leave the lineup, Mr. Wrigley wrote a personal press release.

"As Ernie Banks and many other members of the Chicago Cubs organization are being besieged with questions from the press, television, and radio on an almost hourly basis, this statement is being issued in an effort to clarify the situation, which boils down to the following:

"For more than seven seasons, Ernie has been carrying the team, and except for one brief stretch, he has been continuously in the lineup ever since he joined the club in September of 1953.

"As everyone knows, he played in 717 consecutive games until he recently went to the bench. He had kept his streak going despite injuries and out of pure determination and desire to help the team.

"All this has built up a terrific strain and has meant that he hasn't had an opportunity to take care of a couple of relatively small physical things which have been bothering him, but which he never complained about.

"As Ernie is recognized as one of the greatest players in the majors, as well as a loyal and hardworking team man, the primary interest of the Chicago Cubs is keeping his career going as long as possible. At 30, he has many good years ahead of him, and we hope and expect to have him with us for a long time.

"Therefore, we are trying to cooperate with Ernie in taking off some of the strain, as we do not feel that it is helpful either to the individual or the organization to have one player carrying the whole responsibility for the team.

"Fortunately, we have Ernie Banks, an outstanding team player who also has marvelous team spirit. Ernie knows he has been pressing in an effort to live up to the saying: 'As Banks goes, so go the Cubs.'

"He also recognizes that a little rest and relaxation is the best way to get back on the track as soon as possible.

"Ernie will, therefore, rejoin the team as soon as he has completed getting some further advice on his minor eye trouble. He understands perfectly that he is to take his own time in getting back in stride and in his regular place in the lineup. In line with the idea of taking it easy, he may, for a little while, devote his time to pinch-hitting and helping with batting instruction for some of the younger players.

"We believe that the outlook is that he will be a key player with the Chicago Cubs for many years to come."

That is what the man said, and the man is both my boss and booster: Philip Knight Wrigley.

I'm happy to say that my aches and pains improved enough to let me play 138 of the Cubs' 154 games that season.

Mr. Wrigley is the main reason why so many players are unhappy after they have been traded away from the Cubs. Tony Taylor cried like a baby when he learned that he had been traded to the Phillies in 1960. He even threatened to quit the game. He didn't, but I'm pretty sure I can give you the one word answer he would give if asked to name his favorite baseball city—Chicago. And Tony has had some excellent seasons for the Phillies.

In June 1969 Adolfo Phillips said he was "happy to get away" from the Cubs when he figured in a three-team swap among the Cubs, the Los Angeles Dodgers and the Montreal Expos. I think this was probably Adolfo's immediate reaction to the shock of being traded. Adolfo was always popular with the fans in Wrigley Field, and I'm certain he would welcome a return to the Cubs.

Mr. Wrigley makes sure no player is ever short-changed when he plays for the Cubs. During their prime as young pitchers, both Moe Drabowsky and Dick Drott reaped some very hefty financial returns in the form of incentive pay from the Cubs. Countless other players have too, including Ernie Banks.

Johnny Callison, who was traded to the Cubs from the Phillies after the 1969 season, said he had to come to Chicago to learn something new in the player-owner relationship—and he has been in the majors since 1958!

The Cubs invited Johnny to their winter press conference. During the conference, he and Mr. Holland discussed his 1970 contract. Since this is Johnny's story, I'll let him tell it:

"I visited with Mr. Holland for less than five minutes when we agreed and shook hands on a set salary. We were talking about some other items, such as spring training and housing in Chicago during the regular season, when Mr. Holland said, 'John, I'm going to sweeten our original figure by $500 because that's the way Mr. Wrigley would want it.'

"I've dickered for some contracts in my time, some of them pretty tough, but this is the first time I ever received an increase during the same meeting. I know I'm going to enjoy playing in Chicago for the Cubs."

One of Mr. Wrigley's favorite stories in connection with holdout players concerns Bill Jurges, a great shortstop for the Cubs in the 1930s. Every February, as spring training drew near, Jurges would end up as the Cubs' last unsigned player. When other members of the Cubs' official family could not make progress with Jurges, he would ask for a meeting with Mr. Wrigley. Within a few minutes he and Wrigley always agreed on a figure and Billy reached for a pen as rapidly as he could scoop up a well-hit grounder.

At their Diamond Dinner in 1954, the Chicago baseball writers presented Mr. Wrigley with the annual J. Louis Comiskey memorial plaque for long and meritorious service to baseball.

162

During the dinner, a telegram arrived from Jurges. Showing me the congratulatory message, Mr. Wrigley said, "Ernie, the best I can wish for you is a career as productive as Billy Jurges'. He fought hard for the dollar at the conference table, but he fought a lot harder on the field. A one-day headache, yes, but always a season-long pleasure to watch playing shortstop."

The best example of Wrigley loyalty involves Charley Grimm. Jolly Cholly has managed the Cubs three different times. His first stint ran from 1932 to 1938, the second from 1944 to 1949 and the third was in 1960.

When Mr. Wrigley became alarmed about Charley's failing health, he arranged one of the most bizarre managerial trades in baseball history. At the time, Lou Boudreau and the late Jack Quinlan were the Cubs' radio team for station WGN in Chicago. In Mr. Wrigley's surprising maneuver, Boudreau moved from the radio booth to the field to become the new non-playing manager of the Cubs. Grimm moved into the radio booth as Quinlan's new partner on the air lanes.

Mr. Wrigley has gone to the Cubs' ranks five times to pick a manager for the team. Rogers Hornsby was replaced by Grimm in 1932. Gabby Hartnett was Grimm's successor in 1938. Other former players-turned-pilots were Phil Cavarretta, Stan Hack and Bob Scheffing, the late Johnny Murphy's successor as general manager of the New York Mets.

Since his father, the late William Wrigley, Jr., enticed Joe McCarthy to move from Louisville to Chicago in 1926, the Cubs have had just four "outside" managers: Jimmy Wilson, Frank Frisch, Lou Boudreau and Leo Durocher.

After Jackie Robinson's breaking of the color line, when it was fashionable as well as profitable for some major-league teams to rush and sign a black player, Mr. Wrigley didn't. He wisely refused to be put in the position of signing a black athlete mainly to prime the turnstiles.

Whenever his critics prodded him about his slowness in signing a black player for the Cubs, he simply said, "The Chicago Cubs refuse to sign a Negro player just because it's the thing to do at this time. Our scouts are beating the bushes looking for the young Negro player who can play for the Cubs on merit as a credit to himself as well as the club.

"Just as soon as a player or players are found with this ability, we will attempt to sign them and bring them to Wrigley Field immediately."

Gene Baker from the Kansas City Monarchs and Jim Gilliam from the Baltimore Elite Giants were the first black players of note sought by the Cubs. Baker was signed, but Gilliam returned to the Elite Giants— a move I'll always feel was a great break for me. Had the Cubs kept Gilliam, there would not have been any reason to sign Banks.

Mr. Wrigley made sure before playing us that Gene and I would not be embarrassed by not being ready for the majors. Baker was given every chance to prove himself in the farm system, and the Cubs didn't make any move toward buying my contract from the Kansas City Monarchs until their scouts and some of their coaches rated me a strong major-league prospect.

When I talk about wanting to help the Cubs win a pennant, I have Mr. Wrigley in mind. Nobody in sports deserves a winner more.

At President Nixon's baseball reception at the White House before the 1969 All-Star game in Washington, D.C., Bob Carpenter, owner of the Philadelphia Phillies, was talking about the Cubs' chances of winning the National League pennant.

"If the Phillies can't win," Carpenter said, "I'm pulling for the Cubs because of just one man—Phil Wrigley. He's one pioneer who puts baseball ahead of everything—his team, his hopes. If something isn't good for the complete game, you'll never sell it to him. A man with such ideals deserves nothing but the best, and in Phil's case that would be a pennant."

Saturday, August 15, 1964, was Ernie Banks Day in Wrigley Field. It would take two, and possibly three, lifetimes to repay Mr. Phil Wrigley and all the people involved for my day of days.

Mr. Wrigley petitioned his good friend Philip R. Clarke, a millionaire sportsman in Chicago, to chair a blue-ribbon committee in charge of all arrangements. Mr. Clarke chose distinguished committee members: John A. Barr, chairman of the board of directors of Montgomery Ward & Co.; Tilden Cummings, president of Continental Illinois Bank & Trust Co.; Dr. J. Roscoe Miller, president of Northwestern University; Federal

Judge James B. Parsons; Lenox R. Lohr, president of the Museum of Science & Industry, and chain-store moguls Franklin T. Lunding and Gardner H. Stern.

Wendell Smith, a former sportswriter in Chicago, who had become a member of WGN's television family, was also a member of the committee. Wendell had had a longtime friendship with Jackie Robinson, dating from his days as a baseball writer, and he had also been especially helpful to Gene Baker and me when we first reported to the Cubs.

Rip Collins, a former longtime first baseman and then a member of the Cubs' publicity-promotion department, was the program's coordinator. The fund raising revenue all came from the sale of colorful lapel buttons at 25 cents apiece and the proceeds were to be given to the underprivileged youth of Chicago. This was in keeping with Mr. Wrigley's theory that "fans never should be hit over the head for money to buy gifts for a professional athlete who is paid for his services."

The city-wide lapel sales were so successful that the committee made a $5,000 contribution to the Better Boys Clubs in Chicago in my name. I've always felt the two main needs of youth are leadership and the equipment necessary to allow them to compete in team sports, such as baseball, basketball, football and hockey. The $5,000 gift was spent to buy equipment for the young people in all the poorer communities of Chicago.

With youth the theme for the day, thirty-five hundred Little Leaguers—all dressed in their colorful baseball uniforms—formed a semicircle around the infield for a twenty-two minute pregame program. It was a sight you had to see to believe. If you did see it, I'm sure you will never forget it. I know I won't. Looking at the Little Leaguers, I thought with a laugh, the Detroit Colts often didn't draw this many people in ten games!

As Mr. Clarke launched the program, he said, "We are saluting Ernie Banks with stirring words as not only one of the all-time greats in baseball, but also as a great American."

Suddenly I was thinking of everything: my parents, my family, Dallas, Amarillo, Kansas City, the Cubs and my good life in Chicago. My father had come for the day. All during the program I tried to focus on his reactions. He, like me, had never seen anything like this, not even in his dreams.

One of the most unusual gifts I received was a five-foot-high cake decorated with bats and baseballs and topped with a small statue of me. Attached to the cake was a homemade card with 216 signatures, signatures of patients at the Rehabilitation Institute of Chicago. Just think, all those people, their bodies wracked with serious aches and pain, remembering me. I'm not ashamed to say I cried as I read the card.

Another favorite gift came from my Cubs' teammates. It was a huge silver tray with "Mr. Cub" engraved in the center, surrounded by their signatures. It's one thing to be called "Mr. Cub" in the news media and another to be able to enjoy this rating with your teammates.

I also received a plaque from Warren Giles, the

president of the National League, and a trophy from *The Sporting News*, as well as gifts from writers and WGN and WGN-TV in Chicago.

They talk about diamonds being a girl's best friend, but I have fourteen of them that have made me very happy. They are on a ring and they spell out fourteen—my uniform number with the Cubs. The ring was a gift from the Cubs' organization, just added proof that Mr. Wrigley is something more than an employer.

The program, the planning as well as the presentation, proved anew the value of Mr. Wrigley's counsel. During the early stages of the 1960 season, just after I had won my second MVP award, a group had come to me to ask my permission to stage a day in my honor. It was suggested that there would be the customary gifts for the athlete and all the monies collected for the program would go to this group's charity fund. I thanked these people for their interest but declined to support the project until it was cleared by Mr. Wrigley. It was never mentioned again.

One of the biggest surprises in my life came over the telephone. It was in July 1967. Some news reporters covering City Hall called to get my reaction to a proposal Alderman John Hoellen had offered on the floor of the City Council.

"How does it involve me?" I wanted to know. I hadn't heard anything about it. Apparently, Alderman Hoellen had proposed to substitute a statue of Ernie Banks for Pablo Picasso's gift to the city of Chicago!

Bit by bit the details unfolded. Alderman Hoellen

was unhappy with the 160-ton abstract metal sculpture by Picasso and asked the council to table Mayor Richard J. Daley's resolution to erect the five-story statue in Chicago's new civic center. In its place Alderman Hoellen suggested a five-story statue of Ernie Banks—to provide a "living symbol of a vibrant city."

What could I say? There was Picasso on one side of the debate and me on the other. I just hoped it would be settled to everybody's satisfaction.

The Chicago newspapers gave the story big play, especially when Alderman Hoellen appeared on Chicago TV a night or two later and said of the sculpture, "I call it Picasso's fiasco, a rising heap of rusting iron."

Finally, the City Council supported Mayor Daley's resolution—the Picasso gift was dedicated the following August 15.

11

No Way!

In an era of initials, I have to think of 1969 as the Cubs' D.D. year—the year of Double Depression. A threatened major-league players strike dampened our spirits at the start of the season, and the Mets' success kept us down at the end.

The strike threat was more damaging than you might think. When the Major League Players Association made demands for increased benefits for the players' pension fund, everyone took sides in the bitter debates that followed. I doubt that the things said during the exchange of charges and countercharges will ever be completely forgotten. In the long run, the strike threat did more to hurt the overall player image than it did to harm organized baseball itself. Even though the question was settled without much loss of practice time, teammate relationships changed and some of the scars still show.

Early in the year, most of the Cubs were assembled in Scottsdale, waiting for the all-clear signal. Although everybody felt that the threatened strike would not come off, the apprehension on the field and in the clubhouse was anything but easy on our frayed nerves.

Once agreement was reached between the players' association and the club owners, the Cubs' vice president John Holland made an unprecedented move. He called Ferguson Jenkins, Ron Santo, Billy Williams and me into individual conferences, offering each of us a new two-year contract. Holland batted 4-for-4, but our uncertainty and uneasiness didn't vanish immediately.

We practiced for our first exhibition game, scheduled for March 7 against the San Francisco Giants, in Scottsdale Stadium. Our pitchers had lost all of their early drill time waiting for the settlement, and our only comfort was in knowing that other teams suffered the same setback. We weren't setting any records getting into gear for what later proved to be our greatest season.

We lost our first four spring games, won one and then lost four more in a row before we moved into Tempe on March 18 to play the expansion-born Seattle Pilots. Their lackluster one-and-eight record at least gave us some encouragement.

Leo Durocher had returned to Chicago for a St. Patrick's Day speaking engagement, so coach Pete Reiser took charge of the club. During batting practice in the Pilots' new park, where the Cubs were making their first appearance, Glenn Beckert yelled, "OK, guys, we're going to cut this losing stuff now!" and he moved into the batting cage and immediately hit half a dozen drives to the opposite field.

Watching Glenn, Reiser yelled, "Shake it up! How about some of you fellows trying Glenn's specialty?"

Beckert's enthusiasm swept the club. You could feel the confidence everywhere. Randy Hundley hit a lead-off home run against the Pilots to ignite a four-run fourth inning for the Cubs, and we won the game, 8–5.

The Cubs were on their way, winning eleven of the next seventeen games. We went on to establish a 156-day lease on first place in the National League's Eastern Division and set a new Wrigley Field attendance record of 1,674,993.

Some baseball people attach little importance to winning spring-training games, claiming that emphasis on individual conditioning is the real purpose of training. I'll buy that, but a winning attitude sure helps when things get rough. The way the Cubs opened the official 1969 season is proof of that.

Willie Smith's pinch two-run homer against the Philadelphia Phillies in the eleventh inning gave us a 7–6 opening-day victory. The fans left Wrigley Field shouting, "The Cubs Will Shine in '69!"

From then on we just didn't slow down, taking seven of the first eight home games and advancing on St. Louis in high spirits. When we left, we were even higher. Fergie Jenkins had pitched a five-hitter for a 1–0 victory, and Bill Hands had yielded only three hits to pace our 3–0 triumph the next night.

On April 20, after the first game of a Sunday doubleheader in Montreal, the Cubs had an 11–1 record to top the National League East. Just a month and two days after our turnaround in Tempe, we had won twenty-two out of twenty-nine exhibition and regular season games. I have been with the Cubs when they had some pretty good spurts, but nothing compares with early 1969.

On Billy Williams Day, June 29, we played the St. Louis Cardinals in a Sunday doubleheader before 41,060 fans, our largest home crowd of the season. In the first game Billy tied Stan Musial's National League record of 895 consecutive games played and broke it in the second. It was a day of happy bedlam as we won both games with Billy pounding out two triples, two doubles and a single.

On Monday, July 14, we played the Mets in Wrigley Field with a pitching duel pitting Bill Hands against Tom Seaver. The crowd numbered 40,252—at 1:30 P.M. on a Monday in the only major-league park without field lights!

Mr. Wrigley once said, "Give the Chicago fans something they want to see, and they'll be there whatever the starting time."

To make it worth their while, we snapped Seaver's eight-game winning streak with a 1–0 victory. Billy Williams assured us our fifty-seventh win and Hands his eleventh by singling home Don Kessinger for the game's only run.

During the next two games on Tuesday and Wednesday the crowd counts were 38,608 and 36,795.

We were playing the Dodgers on Sunday, July 27, when a crowd of 30,291 pushed our home attendance total over the million mark, the earliest in the club's history.

You can see why our failure to win the pennant was so disturbing. Had you told me on July 28 what was going to happen on September 10—the night we lost our lead for the first time, never to regain it—I would have answered with just two words, no way!

In spite of our end-of-the-season slump, we had our fair share of records and personal triumphs in 1969. It was a year to be remembered in many ways.

April 9—Billy Williams hit four doubles to tie a major-league record.

May 13—The Cubs won their third straight shutout, 19–0, from San Diego as Dick Selma pitched a three-hitter and I drove in seven runs, for the first time since August 4, 1955.

May 20—Ken Holtzman pitched a five-hitter, blanking the Dodgers in Los Angeles, 7–0, and extending his consecutive scoreless innings to thirty-three.

May 24—I hit the twelfth grand-slam homer of my career as the Cubs won, 7–5, in San Diego.

June 10—Ken Holtzman became the majors' first ten-game winner as the Cubs beat the Atlanta Braves, 3–1.

June 15—Don Kessinger set a new major-league record of fifty-four consecutive games without an error at shortstop.

July 2—The Cubs won game No. 50 in their first 78 with a 4–2 triumph in Montreal.

August 17—The Cubs captured the 75th victory in their first 120 games with a 3–1 win in San Francisco.

August 19—Ken Holtzman pitched a three-walk, no-hit, no-run game to beat the Atlanta Braves, 3–0, for the Cubs' first no-hitter since Don Cardwell blanked the St. Louis Cardinals, 4–0, on May 15, 1960.

Whether you win or lose, you always remember your team's outstanding games. Some gigantic victories assured the Cubs their best finish since winning the pennant in 1945.

Our first 1969 meeting with the New York Mets was April 25. Don Kessinger, Ron Santo and Fergie Jenkins hit solo homers in Shea Stadium to beat Tom Seaver, 3–1.

As early as April 28, some of the critics were convinced the "new" Cubs had finally arrived. We had just won a 2–1 game from the Phillies in ten innings after Philadelphia loaded the bases in the home half of the tenth with nobody out. Ted Abernathy got the next two batters to ground into force plays at the plate, and then Rick Joseph grounded to Santo. Ronnie threw me a perfect strike for the game-ending out. It had been the kind of game we usually lost, so the victory really made us feel like the team to beat.

We were in Cincinnati on June 13 when the Reds battled with us to an 8–8 tie during the first nine innings. In the tenth we spurted for six runs to blueprint a 14–8 victory.

The date is July 28; the place is Chicago's Wrigley Field. The San Francisco Giants give Juan Marichal a 3–2 lead with a run in the tenth. Juan is just three outs away from his fourteenth victory.

With two out, Marichal yields his first walk of the game to Willie Smith, our pinch hitter. Ready?

Don Kessinger, Glenn Beckert and Billy Williams slam out three straight singles and the Cubs win, 4–3.

It was the first game Marichal had lost in Wrigley Field since 1966. We had sixty-three wins to only thirty-nine losses with an even sixty games remaining. The Cubs' enthusiasm was boundless. No way, we thought, there was just no way we could lose.

I guess our hopes were too high. We played just under .500 the rest of the year with twenty-nine victories and thirty-one losses, giving the strong-finishing New York Mets the opening they needed to begin their sensational sweep.

Now there's no way I can say no regrets.

12

Ernie's All-Stars

Some seasons ago during a long rain delay in Philadelphia, Jack Quinlan, the Cubs' radio announcer, asked if I would come up to his booth and talk a little baseball, meaning that he had time to kill.

Jack, Lou Boudreau—his radio partner who was elected to the Hall of Fame in January 1970—and I talked about almost every phase of baseball. As the rain continued and no move was made to call the game, Jack hit on the idea of having Lou pick an American League team from the best players he had ever seen, while I would cover the National League in the same manner.

Quinlan also suggested that we shouldn't name a teammate, past or present. Since I knew we had plenty of time to discuss the situation, I balked and demanded one exception. I told Jack I had never seen a finer third baseman than Ron Santo, the captain of the Cubs. It would be impossible for me to pick my all-time team and not include him. Jack quickly amended the rules and gave me the go-ahead sign.

I picked my team as though I owned a major-league franchise and wanted the ten most skilled athletes in the National League. Right away I chose Hodges for first base. Gil is a fine gentleman and still one of the toughest competitors I've played against.

Jackie Robinson was my second baseman. I had followed Jackie's career closely since I first met him in 1950, playing with his All-Stars.

Selecting a shortstop wasn't easy. I've played against a lot of outstanding guys, but my final choice was Pee Wee Reese. Pee Wee was always a great defensive player, and he could beat you with his bat whether he was bunting or hitting home runs.

Jack and Lou both agreed with my selection of Santo at third base. Santo's enthusiasm is as important to the Chicago Cubs as are his bat and his glove, and he has a record of throwing accuracy that would be the envy of many pitchers.

I picked Stan Musial for left field. I have few better friends than the St. Louis Cardinals' famous No. 6.

Once, after Stan had retired, when the Cubs were in St. Louis early in the season, I was having trouble hitting my weight. The night after the game Stan came to see me.

"Ernie," he volunteered, "a fellow named Father

Time is forcing you to adjust your swing. You have to learn, as I did, that you can't pull everything anymore. Now you're a split second slower getting the bat around on the pitch—especially on a good fast ball.

"Why don't you cut down your swing and try going to the opposite field instead?

"You won't hit with the same power, but singles and doubles can still help you and the club. Once you can make good contact going to the opposite field, go back to pulling and swinging away as you used to.

"That's what I did, and I'm sure you can make the same adjustment. Good luck, and I'll see you later."

His advice worked perfectly. When I had first joined the Cubs in 1953, I couldn't wait to see Stan hit. Now every time the Cubs play in St. Louis, I try to visit Stan at his restaurant. I'll be forever grateful for his assistance when I was down, both mentally and in the daily batting averages.

For the rest of my outfield I picked Willie Mays for center and Hank Aaron for right. Willie always is kidding me about my optimism. Whenever I tell him the Cubs are going to finish first, he says, "You'd better find yourself a new league for the Cubs to play in, because they sure aren't going to be first in the National League. Forget it."

Nobody has ever ribbed me more about the friendly outblowing winds in Wrigley Field than Aaron. Whenever Hank hears about me hitting a four-bagger when the Cubs are playing at home, he says, "There goes Ernie turning on his favorite windmill again, and it's blowing baseballs right out of the park. I just hope I play long enough for him to turn it on when I'm playing in Wrigley Field with the Braves."

Roy Campanella was my All-Star catcher. I find it hard to believe anyone was happier than I was when Campy was named to the Hall of Fame. When he was playing, nobody was a better friend of young black major leaguers. Campy wasn't bossy, but you could depend on his advice when you asked for it.

I picked Sandy Koufax as my left-handed pitcher and Bob Gibson as my right-handed pitcher. When you talk about tough competitors, I've got to rate Bob and Sandy in a dead heat for first.

When Bob Kennedy was associated with the Chicago Cubs, he often talked about someday being able to manage a team that would clinch the pennant on the Fourth of July so he could go fishing and not return to scout and get ready for the World Series until Labor Day. I have some news for Bob—I think Ernie's All-Stars could do it.

13

The Chance
We Haven't Given

Every day somebody, somewhere, talks about a black manager in the major leagues. Where once such discussion among baseball people was taboo, today the opposite is true. Frank Robinson and Maury Wills are two who have already confessed their managerial ambitions.

I don't think the day is too far off, especially when you consider a trend which brought about some startling changes in the National League last year. The Cincinnati Reds hired Sparky Anderson, a man with very little major-league experience. His first year he led his team to a pennant. The Phillies promoted Frank Lucchesi as their field general after a long career in the minors. The Giants followed suit with Charlie Fox.

The point is, somebody on those three clubs decided their minor leaguers had earned the opportunity.

When I came up to the Cubs in 1953, the National League managers were Charley Grimm, Eddie Stanky, Chuck Dressen, Leo Durocher, Fred Haney, Steve O'Neil and Rogers Hornsby. They brought with them excellent credentials from the major leagues. This is no longer a prerequisite, however. More and more managers will be chosen on the basis of leadership, knowledge of the game and the way they can handle men. Color will cease to be a consideration.

Who will be the first black manager?

There are many outstanding candidates, and the front-runner depends upon where you are when the question is asked. Willie Mays, for example, has been a big favorite with Giants' fans in both New York and San Francisco and will receive more managerial consideration in these two cities than in Atlanta or Baltimore.

Personally, I have always thought Gene Baker possesses the necessary leadership qualifications to become a major-league manager. Gene has great knowledge of baseball, and he is blessed with the kind of attitude and disposition so important to a manager in this new era. He is astute, has good balance and good instincts. He can communicate well with players, umpires, fans, management and all branches of the news media. In the competitive market for the sports dollar it is no longer possible for a manager to take all the bows when his club is winning or hide behind "no comment" when it is losing.

Gene is old enough to have been exposed to some

of the old-timers with hell-for-leather thinking, ever ready to challenge any opposition.

After he left the Kansas City Monarchs, he spent part of his career in the minor leagues, where conditions were frequently just as rugged and tense for a black athlete as they were in the majors. I've often thought the term "players' manager" is overworked, but it wouldn't be in Gene Baker's case. He is too well schooled in leadership.

Although we both reported to the Chicago Cubs on September 14, 1953, we had traveled different routes in getting to Wrigley Field. Baker had worked his way up through the Cubs' farm system, having some remarkable seasons for Stan Hack when he was managing the Cubs-owned Los Angeles Angels in the Pacific Coast League. I had come straight from the Monarchs.

I was very nervous when we took the field for the Cubs' second infield drill that day, but Gene settled me down with calm and confident advice. He had been to spring training with the Cubs that year before going back to Los Angeles for his final season with the Angels, and it was obvious that most of the players respected his ability. They exchanged jests and gibes just as they would have if Gene had been with the club all season.

In 1954 during spring training both of us were fighting for our jobs. Before too long Gene received a letter with a newspaper clipping from a friend back in his hometown of Davenport, Iowa. The clipping quoted manager Phil Cavarretta as saying, "Baker and Banks have earned the right to first consideration as the

Cubs' new second base-shortstop combination. I'll play the two of them until they win or lose their jobs."

When Gene showed me the clipping I was happy enough to swing off the chandelier. But he took a different view and said very matter-of-factly, "It's only March, and things can change completely before opening day. The best thing I can tell you is just keep bearing down and forget you ever read this. That way you won't be disappointed."

We did open the season, and pretty soon sportswriters were calling us the Bingo and Bango twins. Gene was Bango, and I was Bingo.

Then one day in Brooklyn the Cubs lost a heartbreaker to the Dodgers when Gene messed up a defensive play. I could tell he was unhappy, but he rebounded like a real champion. As the sportswriters gathered around him in the clubhouse, Gene said, "Fellows, I'll spare you the trouble of asking the question about what happened. The truth is, I goofed. Just goofed, that's all. I don't know why or how I made the mistake, but I can tell you this much: It won't ever happen again. I'll be right back here tomorrow giving it my best shot."

You could tell from the writers' reactions that they were surprised by Gene's frankness and his refusal to shift the blame. On the way back to the hotel, Gene told me how important he thought it was to always level with writers.

"If you play fair with them," he said, "they will treat you the same way, because their work is as important to them as your work is to you."

The visitors' clubhouse in Ebbets Field was the scene of another situation that showed me Gene's special ability to cope with hard times and still inspire people around him.

After the game it was announced that the Cubs had traded Baker and Dee Fondy, our first baseman, to the Pittsburgh Pirates for Dale Long and Lee Walls. The news hit like a blockbuster, but I was more upset than Gene because I was losing my roommate, adviser and very good friend.

We had dinner together before he left to join the Pirates, and even then he had helpful advice.

"Just remember that trades are part of baseball," Gene said, "and as long as you do, you won't be hurt if it ever happens to you."

It turned out that the trade was a good break for Gene. He finished his playing career with the Pirates, even drawing a World Series share when Pittsburgh won the National League pennant in 1960 and took the classic from the New York Yankees.

Gene later coached for the Pirates, working with Danny Murtaugh, a topnotch manager. He also managed for the Pittsburgh organization in Batavia, New York, and after Pittsburgh signed Bob Bailey to a big bonus contract, Baker was sent to work with him in Columbus, Ohio.

Although Gene was a shortstop during all of his early career, he played some great third base for the Cubs, after starting at second. I can remember when Chicago writers were comparing Gene with Floyd Baker of the Chicago White Sox as an outstanding defensive third baseman. Floyd was called "The Blotter," a nickname he had really earned. I don't remember seeing Floyd play, but I did see Gene at his best, and then he was absolutely amazing.

Who are some of the other candidates I would choose to become the first black manager in the majors?

Bill White most certainly deserves consideration. The same can be said of Jim Gilliam. These are two players who worked their way to the top, and they have excellent insight on player problems, with particular understanding of the younger men coming up for the first time. White has retired to a career in radio and television, and Gilliam is coaching for the Los Angeles Dodgers. Both would make good managers if given the opportunity. Jim has the added qualification of learning under Walter Alston and playing with six pennant winners.

At the super-star level, four men definitely merit managerial consideration: Hank Aaron, Willie Mays, Maury Wills and Frank Robinson. Frank has played for pennant winners in both leagues: the 1961 Cincinnati Reds and the 1966, 1969 and 1970 Baltimore Orioles. He has also spent recent winters managing in Puerto Rico, and you can be sure he will be ready if and when his chance comes.

My other two candidates are Monte Irvin and Elston Howard. I have a lot of pleasant memories from Monte's short stint with the Cubs, and I've always thought he could have developed into a great home-run hitter. He has done a fine job as an administrative aide to Commissioner Bowie Kuhn and because of his diplomacy, I'm sure he would make an outstanding manager.

Elston Howard impressed me the first time we met as teammates with the Kansas City Monarchs. When you consider his progress as a player, you've got to think he would make the same advances as a manager.

All the men I have named—Baker, White, Gilliam, Aaron, Mays, Robinson, Irvin, Wills, Howard—have made contributions above and beyond their playing ability. They have earned respect and demonstrated the importance of good leadership. This is what baseball is all about, and it is the reason I consider all my teammates and my fellow major leaguers as brothers.

What about Ernie Banks as a manager?

I've tried to picture myself as a manager. Sometimes I like the idea. Sometimes I wonder if a person wouldn't be a better manager in the majors if he had first managed in the minors. Luke Appling once said, "The very best way to become a short-term manager is to switch from playing to managing without first having spent some time managing in the minor leagues."

To me, the two jobs are as different as day and night. A successful minor-league manager, as I see it, doesn't concern himself too much with winning. His job is to develop a player or players who can make it in the majors. He evaluates his personnel to determine the strong and weak points and then goes to work full time on the weak points. In reality, the minor league must encourage greed, that is, the athlete's desire to reap the dollar rewards and recognition awaiting him in the majors.

If I were managing in the minors, I would want to look at every one of my players as a future Cubs' player and determine the work and help he needed to reach that status. The staggering amounts of money all twenty-four major-league clubs spend for player development programs proves the importance of boosting a minor-league player to the majors. The expense is necessary because baseball lacks the same feeder systems at the college level that professional football and basketball enjoy.

As far as I've been able to determine, there just isn't any set way to manage in the majors—and Gil Hodges has proved this for all time. In 1968, Hodges' first year with the Mets, the New York club finished ninth—twenty-four games out of first and only one game from the cellar. The next season, without too many changes, the Mets turned right around and beat everybody in sight: the Cubs in the Eastern Division, the Atlanta Braves for the National League pennant and the Baltimore Orioles in the World Series. Forget that miracle stuff. I've got to credit incentive, momentum, pitching, confidence and pride of performance—all inspired by Hodges' leadership and timing.

Timing in Gil's situation actually was juggling with a platoon pattern. As a result of Gil's platooning, players such as Cleon Jones, Art Shamsky, Ron Swoboda and even Jerry Grote knew in advance when and where they would play, and Hodges was able to use his full squad to the Mets' best advantage.

Such a system may never work again, but Gil made it worth a second shot. Some day soon a black manager will have an opportunity to test his leadership.

14

Looking Back

During my career I have had an opportunity to meet a lot of people in show business: Danny Thomas, Milton Berle, Jeff Chandler and several others. However, one of the most humorous skits I ever watched happened on a baseball field: Jarry Park in Montreal.

It was June 30, 1969, and the game was played under the worst possible weather conditions after a one-hour-and-forty-six-minute rain delay in the first inning—providing the Cubs with plenty of time to kid Don Kessinger about his game-opening home run off Howie Reed. Don doesn't hit too many homers, but this night he rocketed one over the right-field fence.

In fact, we chided him for hitting a ball so high it brought rain.

When play was resumed, I was the Cubs' first batter

in the second inning. I hit a ball to right-center, and it apparently was lost in the dark, damp background. Tony Venzon, the umpire at second base, backed into the outfield, the better to watch the flight of the ball. As I rounded first base I could see Venzon holding up two fingers to indicate a ground-rule double. Stopping at second, I saw manager Leo Durocher charging into the outfield to talk to Tony.

The Durocher-Venzon meeting produced the funniest tableau you ever saw, with Leo waving both arms back and forth over the wire fence and Tony kicking the bottom of the fence. It was an action-packed scene as the two of them continued to wave and kick while they jawed at each other. Nobody in the park could even guess what the dispute was all about until it was explained that Venzon had ruled that the ball went under the fence instead of over it. This made it a ground-rule double officially.

I've been involved in a lot of oddities, but that was the very first time I ever hit a ball under a fence. Tony later said heavy rains had soaked the ground to such an extent that it was easy for the ball to clear its own tunnel under the fence because it was traveling so fast.

It amused me after I hit my five-hundredth home run to read that vice president John Holland said it was "Ernie's 501st, because nobody ever found the tunnel where his homer flowed under the fence in Montreal."

Nevertheless I received credit for half a homer with the ground-rule double.

There is a lot of show business in baseball—especially in connection with the post-season awards dinners in the various major-league cities and in some of the minor-league cities as well.

Commissioner Bowie Kuhn's black-tie party in Washington, D.C., in 1969 to salute baseball's centennial season was one of the biggest and also one of the best I've ever attended. It always will remain very memorable to me because of my election by the Chicago fans as the "Greatest Cub Player of All Time."

In connection with awards I have been a very fortunate person. A high spot of my career was the Chicagoan-of-the-Year award in 1969. This honor was paid me by the Chicago Press Club, which placed my name alongside such outstanding Chicago sportsmen as George Halas, one of professional football's foremost pioneers, and Bill Veeck, president of Chicago's last baseball pennant winner, the 1959 White Sox. Fred Pannwitt was kind enough to say that my participation in community affairs had as much to do with the presentation as my baseball contributions. These were kind as well as welcome words when spoken by a community leader like Mr. Pannwitt, a former president of the Chicago Press Club.

Providing balance in my life off the baseball field I have been honored with directorships in such organizations as the Jackson Park Hospital, LaRabida Sanitarium, Glenwood Home for Boys, Metropolitan YMCA Joint Negro Appeal, Woodlawn Boys Club, Chicago Rehabilitation Institute and The Big Brothers.

A previously scheduled event forced me to miss another outstanding honor—installation as the first Negro in the Texas Sports Hall of Fame. During the 1970 season I promised Eloyce and the children a Christmas trip to Europe regardless of whether the Cubs won or lost the National League Eastern championship. We lost, but we still made the trip to Europe.

This meant I couldn't be in Dallas for the ceremony. Others elected were Max Hirsch (posthumously), Jess Neely and Buster Brannon. Since the days when I first started to read the sports pages, I have followed Mr. Neely's career as a football coach at Rice and Mr. Brannon's basketball teams at both Rice and Texas Christian. Both of these gentlemen were outstanding coaches and produced many of Texas' foremost teams as well as athletes—and history proves there have been a lot of both.

Few awards have pleased me more than my acceptance into the Texas Hall of Fame. It's something I never is hanging in the dining room of my parents' Dallas just can't find words to describe properly. I'm sure you would be in the same position knowing your name was being placed alongside those of such stars as Tris Speaker, Ben Hogan, Babe Didrikson, Sammy Baugh, Bo McMillin, Rogers Hornsby, Byron Nelson, Davey O'Brien, Doak Walker, Dana X. Bible, Bobby Layne, Kyle Rote, Bill Shoemaker, Eddie Dyer and A. J. Foyt. You'll understand what I mean when I tell you that the Hall of Fame's membership "shall be limited to those persons, male or female, living or dead, whose achievements in athletics have brought lasting fame and honor to Texas."

Although my father was too ill to attend, my mother was there along with some of my sisters and brothers. Raymond Hollie, my coach at Booker T. Washington High School in Dallas—he's since moved to Roosevelt—accepted my plaque with these words:

"All his life Ernie Banks has given thanks for being born to a strong mother and father, that he appreciated being born in Dallas and had the opportunity to attend a small school with a good athletic program. Now I'll close saying what I'm sure Ernie would say: 'Thank God I was born in America.'"

Coach Hollie knows, I'm sure, that I couldn't possibly have said it better or with more meaning. My mother was so thrilled that the Hall of Fame plaque still is hanging in the dining room of my parents' Dallas home.

Often I'm asked what particular event in my life I would like to repeat if I had the opportunity. There have been a lot of thrills, but one of the more meaningful events was my post-season trip to Vietnam in 1968 to visit the American troops stationed there.

Bing Devine, general manager of the St. Louis Cardinals, and pitchers Larry Jackson and Pete Richert were members of our group. During the sixteen-day junket we visited countless installations and talked to literally hundreds of servicemen. Sports, especially baseball, are their big interest. They talk shop every chance they get.

Some nights the shelling was so loud we couldn't sleep, but that is the way of life over there. We would fly to some posts, take a boat to others. Toward the end of the trip Richert and I were given a day off to shop or go sight-seeing in a little town. As we moved around, Pete said:

"This is better than a day off in San Diego. At least we know where we can or can't go."

Afterward Pete called it his "greatest experience as a baseball player." I buy that all the way. The servicemen are our real heroes. You feel a lot of pride being an American, and privileged to visit with them when they are so far away from their homes and their families.

I wish it were possible for baseball to arrange two or three such junkets annually to entertain these deserving servicemen. An athlete's work is child's play compared to theirs.

15

It Means a Lot

When you play professional sports, you move around a lot and meet a lot of people. You have some high times you never want to forget, and of course others you would like to cross right off the record books. A lot of people call me "Joy Boy," and I guess it is because my life in baseball has been so filled with pleasure.

Would I do anything differently the second time around? The answer would have to be no. Nothing could replace the fine relationships I've had with the people involved in the game or the fantastic thrills I've felt on and off the field.

These are some of the memories that have made me proud to be a part of professional baseball.

Fans sometimes ask what a first baseman and a runner talk about. As often as not, they just discuss the game or a recent spectacular play; now and then an umpire will tell a good story. I'll always remember, however, the day the Cubs were playing the Dodgers in Wrigley Field and Wes Parker reached first on a single. After the ball was returned to the pitcher, Wes said, "Ernie, I'd like to invite you and your wife out for dinner tomorrow. We'll eat early, because I have tickets for *The Odd Couple,* and I'd like Mr. and Mrs. Banks to be my guests for the evening."

Imagine that! I accepted between pitches.

You read about players saying they would rather rest for three days than play in the annual All-Star game, but I've yet to meet a player who was in an All-Star game and wasn't glad.

Ron Santo, the Cubs' field captain, was wishing he had stayed home when he went to Bloomington, Minnesota, home of the Twins, for the 1965 All-Star game. A third baseman, Santo was the second choice behind the Phillies' Richie Allen, and he was sure he wouldn't get to play much.

Gene Mauch (named to manage the National League team after the late Johnny Keane had moved from the Cardinals to the Yankees) spotted Santo waiting in line to check into the hotel. "There's my type of player," Gene said, "a real hard-nosed competitor. Santo can play for me any time."

Somebody told Ron what Mauch had said, and right away he began to cheer up. The next day it was Santo's single that drove in Willie Mays with the run the Nationals needed to win the game, 6–5. On his way to first, Ron was already thinking about the next All-Star game.

Hank Sauer can recall July 8, 1952, as if it were yesterday. His mighty home run—a drive to the top of the left-field pavilion in old Shibe Park—powered the Nationals to a 3–2 victory. Hank also made it a big day for the Cubs since Bob Rush became the winning pitcher when the game ended because of rain.

One of my favorite All-Star games was the one in Anaheim, California, in 1967. Walter Alston, the National League manager, used me only as a pinch hitter. The rest of the time I stayed in the dugout, cheering the team and observing the Alston strategy firsthand.

They say that Alston is considerate and understanding. This particular day he really lived up to the reputation. He went to a lot of trouble to get as many players as possible into the game and still win it. When it was all over, we had fielded twenty-four players in fifteen innings and won the game, 2–1!

The Dodgers' Claude Osteen was the only player Alston wasn't able to squeeze in, and Osteen was warming up in the bullpen at the finish. There have been some great All-Star games, but the 1967 match had a touch of everything. Three solo homers produced all the runs, and thirty batters struck out—seventeen of them American Leaguers.

When Tony Perez, of the Cincinnati Reds, hit the winning homer in the fifteenth, you would have thought the National League had just won the World Series. I was in the Mets' clubhouse after they beat Baltimore in the 1969 World Series, and the bedlam was unbelievable. Still, I don't think the reactions were any louder or happier than they were that July day in Anaheim.

The 1969 All-Star game in Washington D.C. preceded baseball's centennial celebration and was followed by a White House reception for club owners, executives, players, umpires and representatives of the news media.

Sons of poor black folks from Dallas don't get the opportunity to meet the President of the United States very often. As I shook hands with President Nixon in the receiving line, he said, "Glad to meet you, Ernie Banks. You are the youngest looking thirty-five-year-old first baseman I've ever seen."

Commissioner Bowie Kuhn, who was standing next to the President, interjected, "No, Mr. President, I think Ernie is thirty-eight."

"Well he looks thirty-five," the President answered. "And don't tell any of the other fellows, but this man deserves a pennant—and I hope he gets it."

It was a day packed with memories, and I kept thinking that it just couldn't have happened anywhere but in the United States. Where else could you have found Ted Williams—wearing a sports shirt without a tie—talking hitting with evangelist Billy Graham, while "bankers" Casey Stengel and Stan Musial were discussing interest rates and batting averages? Great pitchers Lefty Grove and Carl Hubbell reviewed the highlights of their spectacular careers, and we heard the President humbly saying, "I never made the team, but I am always awed in the presence of those who did." He recalled a near pick-off play involving Lou Boudreau and Bob Feller in the 1948 World Series and added, "If I had to start all over again, I'd like to be a sportswriter."

I was really proud as I watched President Nixon step down from the podium to greet Roy Campanella in his wheelchair and offer Campy congratulations on his upcoming installation in baseball's Hall of Fame.

I know firsthand that President Nixon's interest in sports extends beyond White House receptions. When Lou Boudreau, who had been a great shortstop-manager for the Cleveland Indians before becoming a member of the Chicago Cubs' radio broadcasting team with station WGN, was voted into baseball's Hall of Fame, he received a telegram from Mr. Nixon.

A short time later, the Chicago Press Club honored me as the Chicagoan-of-the-Year for 1969. During the dinner commemorating the event, the Press Club gave me a medallion, and I also received a telegram of congratulations from the President.

January 1970 was quite an important month in my life. Before the presentation of the Press Club award, I had received a trophy naming me the "Greatest Cub Player of All Time" and a "Mr. Baseball" award from the Milwaukee baseball writers. The all-time Cub award resulted from a poll conducted by Commissioner Kuhn's office in connection with baseball's centennial celebration in 1969.

Awards mean a lot, but they don't say it all. The people in baseball mean more to me than any statistics.

Just before the 1958 season opened, the Cubs

drafted Tony Taylor out of the San Francisco Giants' farm system. A bashful Cuban, Tony wasn't completely happy during his early days with the Cubs. I'll always feel that during his first season in the majors he was overwhelmed by the vast city of Chicago and felt his language problems just made things more bewildering and embarrassing.

Tony told me how homesick he was and how much he wanted to return to his native Havana. I tried to think up ways to cheer him up but wasn't having much luck until I suggested to a sportswriter assigned to the Cubs that we take Tony out to dinner. The writer set a dinner date for the very next night and invited both Tony and me to his home.

When I stopped to pick up Tony at his hotel, he backed off, saying he was too sick to eat. I knew he was bluffing. It was obvious that Tony was still bothered by having so much trouble with his English.

Since Tony wouldn't give in, I went on to the writer's house and reported the situation. He picked up the phone right away. "Ernie is coming back to get you, and you'd better be there," the writer told Tony. "This is your party. You just don't walk out on your friends like that."

Tony came, and after cocktails and steaks, the writer's wife served ice cream covered with green crème de menthe in long-stemmed glasses. Intrigued, Tony asked what the green stuff was.

"That's Notre Dame holy water," the writer answered. "I think you'll like it."

Tony did—the first and second servings. Ever since,

ice cream topped with Notre Dame holy water has been his favorite dessert.

When Tony was traded to the Philadelphia Phillies in 1960, he was heartbroken and suffering through the same slow start with the Phillies that we had seen in Chicago. Somehow, Tony's "holy water" story was relayed to John Quinn, the Phillies' general manager. After a game in Connie Mack Stadium one night, Tony returned to the clubhouse and found a package in his locker with a card reading: "Thought you might enjoy a little Notre Dame holy water after the game. Drink it in good health." It was signed, "A Friend."

The friend, of course, was Mr. Quinn, and a very happy Tony Taylor—now a thirteen-year veteran in the major leagues and going strong—still enjoys telling the holy water story.

I think very few people realize the importance of giving a rookie a pat on the back. It's a tough time at the start of a tough career, and a friendly boost really helps.

Overall, my life has been pretty easy. I haven't had to face many emergencies, and I'm thankful for that, but one incident during spring training in March 1970 was hard to handle.

It was a day like most others. I ate breakfast, went through the newspaper, checked the mail and made the trip to the ball park. After suiting up, running, throwing and the usual pepper games, it was my turn in the batting cage. The customary small talk and kidding was going on around the cage when coach Joe Amalfitano called me aside and said John Holland wanted to see me in the clubhouse.

In the clubhouse I followed Mr. Holland and Joe Becker, another of the Cubs' coaches, into Leo's office. It was then that I began to wonder if I had been traded. At best, I figured the Cubs had decided to go with rookie Roe Skidmore at first base. It didn't seem right that Joe, who worked mainly with the pitchers, would be involved in giving me the bad news, but frankly I didn't know what else to think.

Mr. Holland closed the door and spoke quietly. "Ernie, Joe received a phone call last night, and we want you to know all about it, step by step."

Becker spoke very slowly as if he wanted to be sure I had time to take in each detail. "First off, the operator said Larry Jackson was calling collect. I accepted the call, naturally.

"Then this voice said, 'I've got a rifle, and I'm gunning for Ernie Banks.' Soon as I heard that, I knew it wasn't Larry!

" 'You're out of your mind,' I told him. 'You can't do a thing like that.'

" 'Well, I'll get him, don't worry about that,' he fired back. 'I've got a rifle, and I'm going to use it.' That's when I hung up."

My first reaction was that it was some kind of practical joke, but Holland and Becker didn't look amused. The three of us sat there tense and silent. Finally Mr. Holland started to talk about what steps he planned to take.

Two plainclothesmen from the Scottsdale Police Department arrived, followed by two agents from FBI headquarters in Phoenix. Joe repeated the story. It hit me a lot harder the second time around.

I called my parents in Dallas and my in-laws in Los Angeles. Eloyce's parents thought it might be best to have Eloyce and the three children stay with them, and I agreed. But when I talked to Eloyce, she would hear nothing of leaving. The Cubs arranged for twenty-four-hour security around our Scottsdale apartment, and I stayed indoors for the rest of that day and all of the next.

Bad news travels fast. The twins, Joey and Jerry, knew about the phone call before they got home from school. They were obviously upset, but they relaxed when they realized that for a change I would be home with them full time.

The following week the FBI made an arrest in Chicago, but not before the Cubs had had to arrange security for Ron Santo's home in the Chicago suburbs. Ronnie had also received threatening calls and naturally was worried about his wife, Judy, and their children.

After that, all the phone calls to players living at the Ramada Inn, the Cubs' official headquarters in Scottsdale, were monitored and arrangements were made for added security when the Cubs were on the road.

It's a good feeling to know that you've got an organization like the Cubs to back you up when you're in trouble. I'll never forget the way they responded to the threats on my life and Santo's. It meant a lot to me then, and it means a lot now.

Since the Scottsdale incident, I've stayed away from crowds whenever possible. Autographs are part of the game, and I'm glad to give mine to anyone who asks for it. Nevertheless, I think that these days athletes should have more than a healthy respect for the fans' behavior. You never know what is going to trigger violence.

The unruly conduct of some people watching the Cubs' 1970 home opener wasn't really unexpected. We had seen their fervor building toward frenzy at the end of the previous season. I don't think people realize how involved they are in sports. Sports are a way to let off steam, and when a crowd is swept away, you can't tell what will happen. I wish it weren't true, but today the professional athlete needs protection from the public.

I worry about young people when I look at their lives filled with tension and so many difficult decisions. I'm not sure they enjoy being young—and this spells trouble. I'm glad my children love sports. Sports will keep them healthy and help them learn the importance of cooperation and friendship. I hope in some way I'm reaching other kids, too, and that some of them will discover the wonderful opportunities offered by baseball and other sports on both professional and amateur levels.

Ernie Banks'
Lifetime
Statistics

LIFETIME BOX SCORE

Year Club	L	Pos.	G	AB	R	H	2B	3B	HR	RBI	BA	PO	A	E	FA
1953—Chi.	Nat.	SS	10	35	3	11	1	1	2	6	.314	19	33	1	.981
1954—Chi.	Nat.	SS	•154	593	70	163	19	7	19	79	.275	312	475	34	.959
1955—Chi.	Nat.	SS	•154	596	98	176	29	9	44	117	.295	290	482	22	*.972
1956—Chi.	Nat.	SS	139	538	82	160	25	8	28	85	.297	279	357	25	.962
1957—Chi.	Nat.	SS-3B	•156	594	113	169	34	6	43	102	.285	241	348	14	.977
1958—Chi.	Nat.	SS	*154	*617	119	193	23	11	*47	*129	.313	292	468	•32	.960
1959—Chi.	Nat.	SS	•155	589	97	179	25	6	45	*143	.304	271	*519	12	*.985
1960—Chi.	Nat.	SS	*156	597	94	162	32	7	*41	117	.271	*283	*488	18	*.977
1961—Chi.	Nat.	S-O-1B	138	511	75	142	22	4	29	80	.278	273	370	21	.968
1962—Chi.	Nat.	*1B-3B	154	610	87	164	20	6	37	104	.269	*1462	*107	11	.993
1963—Chi.	Nat.	1B	130	432	41	98	20	1	18	64	.227	1178	78	9	.993
1964—Chi.	Nat.	1B	157	591	67	156	29	6	23	95	.264	*1565	*132	10	.994
1965—Chi.	Nat.	1B	163	612	79	162	25	3	28	106	.265	*1682	93	15	.992
1966—Chi.	Nat.	1B-3B	141	511	52	139	23	7	15	75	.272	1183	92	13	.990
1967—Chi.	Nat.	1B	151	573	68	158	26	4	23	95	.276	*1383	*91	10	.993
1968—Chi.	Nat.	1B	150	552	71	136	27	0	32	83	.246	1379	88	6	.996
1969—Chi.	Nat.	1B	155	565	60	143	19	2	23	106	.253	*1419	87	4	*.997
1970—Chi.	Nat.	1B	72	222	25	56	6	2	12	44	.252	528	35	4	.993
Major League Totals			2489	9338	1301	2567	405	90	509	1630	.275	14039	4343	261	.986

* Best in Major Leagues
• Best in National League

ALL-STAR GAME RECORD

Year League	Pos.	AB	R	H	2B	3B	HR	RBI	BA	PO	A	E	FA
1955—National	SS	2	0	0	0	0	0	0	.000	2	1	0	1.000
1957—National	SS	3	0	1	0	0	0	1	.333	0	3	0	1.000
1958—National	SS	3	0	0	0	0	0	0	.000	2	3	1	.833
1959—National (both games)	SS	7	1	2	2	0	0	0	.286	3	2	1	.833
1960—National (both games)	SS	7	2	3	1	0	1	2	.429	4	5	0	1.000
1961—National (second game)	SS	1	0	0	0	0	0	0	.000	0	0	0	.000
1962—National (both games)	1B	4	1	1	0	1	0	0	.250	5	2	0	1.000
1965—National	1B	4	0	2	0	0	0	0	.500	11	0	0	1.000
1967—National	PH	1	0	1	0	0	0	0	1.000	0	0	0	.000
1969—National	PH	1	0	0	0	0	0	0	.000	0	0	0	.000
All-Star Game Totals		33	4	10	3	1	1	3	.303	27	16	2	.956

Member of National League All-Star team in 1956 game; did not play.
Player-Coach, Chicago Cubs, 1967 through 1970.

Records Held

Major-League Records

Most consecutive games played from start of major league career (424), September 17, 1953, through August 10, 1956.

Most home runs by a shortstop, season (47), 1958.

Highest fielding percentage by a shortstop, season (.985), 1959.

Fewest errors by a shortstop, season (12), 1959.

Tied Major-League Records

Most grand-slam home runs, season (5), May 11 and 29, July 17, August 2 and September 19, 1955.

Most games by a first basemen during a 162-game season (162), 1965.

Most sacrifice flies, game (3), June 2, 1961.

Most put-outs by a first baseman, game (22), May 9, 1963.

Most three-base hits, game (3), June 11, 1966.

National League Records

Most seasons leading in games played (6).

National League Statistics Leader

1958—Slugging percentage (.614). Total bases (379).

1960—Double plays by a shortstop (64).

1962—Double plays by a first baseman (134).

Awards

The *Sporting News* Outstanding National League Player, 1958–59.

Most Valuable Player, National League, 1958–59.

Shortstop, *Sporting News* All-Star team, 1955–58–59–60.

Shortstop, *Sporting News* All-Star fielding team, 1960.

National League All-Star, 1955–56–57–58–59–60–61–62–65–67–69.

Ernie Banks' Club Career Records

Banks		Runner-up	
GAMES	2,489*	Phil Cavarretta	1,953
AT-BATS	9,338*	Stan Hack	7,278
RUNS	1,301	Stan Hack	1,239
HITS	2,567	Stan Hack	2,193
DOUBLES	405	Gabby Hartnett	391
HOME RUNS	509*	Billy Williams	291
TOTAL BASES	4,679*	Billy Williams	3,179
RUNS BATTED IN	1,630*	Gabby Hartnett	1,153
EXTRA BASE HITS	1,004*	Gabby Hartnett	686

* Since 1900.

The Chicago Cubs' Over 30 Homer Club

Ernie Banks				Billy Williams	
1958 —	47	1949 —	31	1970 —	42
1959 —	45	1951 —	30	1965 —	34
1955 —	44	**Hack Wilson**		1964 —	33
1957 —	43	1930 —	56	1968 —	30
1960 —	41	1929 —	39	**Rogers Hornsby**	
1962 —	37	1928 —	31	1929 —	40
1968 —	32	1927 —	30	**Andy Pafko**	
Hank Sauer		**Ron Santo**		1950 —	36
1954 —	41	1965 —	33	**Gabby Hartnett**	
1952 —	37	1967 —	31	1930 —	37
1950 —	32	1964 —	30	**Bill Nicholson**	
		1966 —	30	1944 —	33

Ernie Banks' Career Grand-Slam Home Runs

Date	Pitcher	Club	Inning	Site
May 11, 1955	Meyer	Brooklyn	1	Wrigley Field
May 29, 1955	Burdette	Milwaukee	3	Wrigley Field
June 17, 1955	Negray	Philadelphia*	6	Wrigley Field
August 2, 1955	Littlefield	Pittsburgh	5	Wrigley Field
Sept. 19, 1955	McDaniel	St. Louis	6	Sportsman's Park
May 13, 1959	Purkey	Cincinnati	3	Wrigley Field
August 29, 1959	Spahn	Milwaukee	3	Wrigley Field
April 14, 1960	Sanford	San Francisco	3	Candlestick Park
May 28, 1961	Miller	San Francisco	8	Wrigley Field
Sept. 27, 1964	Bolin	San Francisco#	5	Wrigley Field
July 7, 1968	Blass	Pittsburgh*	1	Wrigley Field
May 24, 1969	Baldschun	San Diego	5	San Diego Stadium

* —first game of doubleheader
\# —second game of doubleheader

212

Box scores from games in which Ernie Banks hit his 1st, 100th, 200th, 300th, 400th and 500th home runs.

Home Run No. 1—Sept. 20, 1953

At St. Louis

Cubs (6)	AB	R	H	RBI		Cardinals (11)	AB	R	H	RBI
Baumholtz, cf	5	1	2	1		Repulski, cf	5	1	1	0
Miksis, 2b	5	1	2	0		Hemus, ss	4	3	2	2
Fondy, 1b	5	0	1	0		Musial, lf	4	4	3	3
Kiner, lf	4	3	1	0		Slaughter, rf	5	0	0	2
Sauer, rf	5	0	1	1		Schoendienst, 2b	3	2	3	2
Serena, 3b	5	0	2	1		Jablonski, 3b	4	0	2	1
Banks, ss	4	1	3	3		Castiglione, 3b	0	0	0	0
Garagiola, c	4	0	1	0		Bilko, 1b	4	0	0	1
Hacker, p	1	0	0	0		Rand, c	4	0	2	0
Lown, p	0	0	0	0		Staley, p	3	1	2	0
Cavarretta, ph	1	0	1	0		Brazle, p	0	0	0	0
Elston, p	0	0	0	0		White, p	0	0	0	0
Baker, ph	1	0	0	0						
Leonard, p	0	0	0	0		Totals	36	11	15	11
Sawatski, ph	1	0	0	0						
Moisan, p	0	0	0	0						
Totals	41	6	14	6						

Chicago	011	101	011 — 6
St. Louis	203	402	00x —11

E—(none); DP—Chicago 1, St. Louis 1; LOB—Chicago 9, St. Louis 5
3B—Musial, Banks, Hemus 2, Serena
HR—Baumholtz, Musial, Schoendienst, Banks
S—Staley

Pitching Summary

	IP	H	R	ER	BB	SO
Hacker (L, 11–19)	2-1/3	7	5	5	2	1
Lown	1-2/3	4	4	4	1	0
Elston	2	3	2	2	0	1
Leonard	1	1	0	0	0	2
Moisan	1	0	0	0	0	0
Staley (W, 18–8)	8	11	5	5	1	2
Brazle	1/3	2	1	1	0	0
White	2/3	1	0	0	0	1

U—Secory, Dascoli, Dixon; T—2:13; A—(paid) 8,569

213

Home Run No. 100—June 9, 1957
(First Game)

At Philadelphia

Cubs (7)	AB	R	H	RBI		Phillies (3)	AB	R	H	RBI
Morgan, 2b	4	1	1	0		Ashburn, cf	5	1	2	2
Speake, lf	2	2	0	0		Hamner, 2b	5	0	0	0
Banks, 3b	3	2	1	3		Lopata, c	5	0	2	1
Long, 1b	4	1	1	1		Bouchee, 1b	3	0	1	0
Moryn, rf	4	1	2	2		Jones, 3b	2	0	0	0
Bolger, rf	0	0	0	0		Repulski, lf	4	0	1	0
Tanner, cf	3	0	0	1		Fernandez, ss	4	1	2	0
Walls, cf	0	0	0	0		Cardwell, p	1	1	0	0
Neeman, c	4	0	0	0		Roberts, p	1	0	1	0
Littrell, ss	4	0	0	0		Hemus, ph	0	0	0	0
Drott, p	3	0	0	0			—	—	—	—
Lown, p	0	0	0	0		Totals	34	3	9	3
Totals	31	7	5	7						

Chicago	000	000	331 — 7	
Philadelphia	003	000	000 — 3	

E—Ashburn; DP—Chicago 2; LOB—Chicago 1, Philadelphia 9
2B—Lopata, Fernandez 2, Ashburn, Moryn
HR—Banks (7)
SB—Lopata, Morgan
SF—Tanner

Pitching Summary

	IP	H	R	ER	BB	SO
Drott (W, 4-6)	9-1/3	9	3	3	4	7
Lown	2/3	0	0	0	0	2
*Cardwell	6	2	3	3	2	7
Roberts (L, 6-7)	3	3	4	3	1	0

* Faced 3 batters in 7th.
HBP—by Drott, Cardwell; U—Donatelli, Delmore, Smith, Conlan; T—2:37

Home Run No. 200—June 14, 1959

At Chicago

Braves (0)	AB	R	H	RBI		Cubs (6)	AB	R	H	RBI
Wise, 2b	3	0	0	0		T. Taylor, 2b	3	1	3	0
Mathews, 3b	4	0	1	0		Dark, 3b	3	1	1	0
Aaron, rf	4	0	1	0		Walls, rf	4	1	2	3
Covington, lf	4	0	1	0		Banks, ss	4	1	1	2
Torre, 1b	4	0	0	0		Long, 1b	4	1	2	1
Bruton, cf	4	0	2	0		Thomas, lf	4	0	0	0
Crandall, c	3	0	0	0		Altman, cf	4	0	1	0
Logan, ss	4	0	1	0		S. Taylor, c	3	1	1	0
Rush, p	2	0	1	0		Drott, p	4	0	0	0
Roach, ph	1	0	0	0			—	—	—	—
Willey, p	0	0	0	0		Totals	33	6	11	6
Vernon, ph	1	0	0	0						
	—	—	—	—						
Totals	34	0	7	0						

Milwaukee	000	000	000 — 0
Chicago	002	100	30x — 6

E—(None); DP—Milwaukee 1; LOB—Milwaukee 9, Chicago 6
2B—T. Taylor, Covington, Long, S. Taylor, Walls, Bruton, Altman
HR—Long, Banks
S—Dark

Pitching Summary

	IP	H	R	ER	BB	SO
Rush (L, 4–3)	6	8	3	3	2	4
Willey	2	3	3	3	0	1
Drott (W, 1–0)	9	7	0	0	2	3

U—Boggess, Gorman, Landes; T—2:25; A—36,895

Home Run No. 300—April 18, 1962

At Chicago

Astros (2)	AB	R	H	RBI		Cubs (3)	AB	R	H	RBI
Aspromonte, 3b	3	1	1	1		White, ss	3	1	1	1
Amalfitano, 2b	4	0	1	0		Hubbs, 2b	5	0	1	0
Gernert, 1b	4	0	1	0		Williams, lf	5	0	1	0
Mejias, rf	5	0	1	0		Banks, 1b	5	1	4	2
Pendleton, lf	4	0	1	1		Santo, 3b	4	0	1	0
Smith, c	3	0	0	0		McKnight, rf	4	0	1	0
Heist, cf	4	1	2	0		Altman, cf	4	0	1	0
Buddin, ss	3	0	1	0		Thacker, c	3	0	2	0
Woodeshick, p	2	0	0	0		Brock, ph	0	1	0	0
Farrell, p	1	0	0	0		Barrangan, c	0	0	0	0
						Will, ph	1	0	0	0
Totals	33	2	8	2		S. Taylor, c	0	0	0	0
						Ellsworth, p	4	0	0	0
						Totals	38	3	12	3

Houston	000	110	000	0 — 2
Chicago	100	000	100	1 — 3

E—(None); DP—Houston 2, Chicago 2; LOB—Houston 8, Chicago 8
2B—Altman
3B—Banks (2)
HR—Banks
SB—Brock; S—Woodeshick, Smith; SH—Aspromonte

Pitching Summary

	IP	H	R	ER	BB	SO
*Woodeshick	7	11	2	2	1	4
**Farrell (L, 0–2)	2-2/3	1	1	1	0	3
Ellsworth (W, 1–0)	11	8	2	2	4	2

* Faced 2 batters in 8th. ** Two out in 10th when winning run scored.
HBP—by Woodeshick (White); WP—Woodeshick; U—Walsh, Conlan, Burkhart; T—2.25; A—3,318

Home Run No. 400—Sept. 2, 1965

At Chicago

Cardinals (3)	AB	R	H	RBI	Cubs (5)	AB	R	H	RBI
Brock, lf	4	1	1	1	Landrum, cf	3	0	0	1
Flood, cf	4	0	0	0	Beckert, 2b	5	1	2	0
Groat, ss	4	0	1	0	Williams, lf	4	1	2	1
Boyer, 3b	4	1	1	0	Santo, 3b	3	1	1	0
White, 1b	4	1	1	0	Banks, 1b	2	1	1	3
Javier, 2b	3	0	0	0	Kuenn, lf	4	0	1	0
Francona, ph	1	0	0	0	Clemens, pr-lf	0	0	0	0
McCarver, c	4	0	2	1	Krug, c	3	1	0	0
Shannon, rf	3	0	0	0	Kessinger, ss	3	0	2	0
Skinner, ph	1	0	0	0	Hendley, p	2	0	0	0
Simmons, p	1	0	0	0	Abernathy, p	0	0	0	0
Gagliano, ph	1	0	0	0					
Dennis, p	0	0	0	0	Totals	29	5	9	5
Savage, ph	0	0	0	0					
Briles, p	0	0	0	0					
Woodeshick, p	0	0	0	0					
Totals	34	3	6	2					

St. Louis	000	110	100 — 3
Chicago	004	100	00x — 5

E—Flood, Kessinger, Banks, Santo; DP—St. Louis 1, Chicago 1; LOB—St. Louis 5, Chicago 9
2B—Williams
HR—Brock (14), Banks (24)
S—Hendley, Abernathy; SH—Landrum

Pitching Summary

	IP	H	R	ER	BB	SO
Simmons (L, 9–13)	4	6	5	5	3	5
Dennis	2	1	0	0	1	0
Briles	1-1/3	2	0	0	1	0
Woodeshick	2/3	0	0	0	0	0
Hendley (W, 2–2)	7-1/3	6	3	2	1	2
Abernathy (Save)	1-2/3	0	0	0	0	2

HBP—by Dennis (Kessinger); T—2:24; A—(paid) 5,104

Home Run No. 500—May 12, 1970

At Chicago

Braves (3)	AB	R	H	RBI		Cubs (4)	AB	R	H	RBI
Jackson, ss	4	1	0	0		Kessinger, ss	5	1	3	0
Millan, 2b	5	1	1	0		Beckert, 2b	5	0	1	0
Aaron, rf	4	0	0	0		Williams, lf	4	1	1	1
Carty, lf	3	0	3	0		Santo, 3b	5	1	2	1
Garr, ph	0	0	0	0		Callison, rf	4	0	0	0
Wilhelm, p	0	0	0	0		Banks, 1b	3	1	1	2
King, ph	1	0	0	0		Hickman, cf	3	0	0	0
Priddy, p	0	0	0	0		Martin, c	2	0	0	0
Cepeda, 1b	4	0	0	0		Hall, ph	1	0	0	0
Boyer, 3b	4	1	2	0		Hiatt, c	1	0	1	0
Gonzalez, cf	4	0	0	0		Holtzman, p	2	0	0	0
Tillman, c	2	0	0	0		Smith, ph	1	0	0	0
Lum, lf	1	0	0	0		Abernathy, p	0	0	0	0
Jarvis, p	3	0	0	0		Popovich, ph	1	0	0	0
Didier, c	1	0	0	0		Regan, p	0	0	0	0
Totals	36	3	6	0		Totals	37	4	9	4

Braves	200	000	100	00	—	3
Chicago	010	000	101	01	—	4

E—Martin; DP—Braves 1, Cubs 2; LOB—Braves 4, Cubs 6
2B—Boyer, Santo
HR—Banks (3), Williams (12)
SF—Banks

Pitching Summary

	IP	H	R	ER	BB	SO
Jarvis	8	4	2	2	1	6
Wilhelm	2	2	1	1	0	2
*Priddy (L, 2–2)	0	3	1	1	1	0
Holtzman	8	5	3	2	3	4
Abernathy	2	1	0	0	0	0
Regan (W, 2–0)	1	0	0	0	1	0

* Faced 4 batters in 11th.
WP—Holtzman 3; U—Venzon, Secory, Engel, Wendelstedt; T—2:45; A—(paid) 5,264

ERNIE BANKS' HOME RUNS BY PARKS

(First 500 home runs: complete through game of May 12, 1970)

YEAR	CHICAGO Wrigley Field	CINCI. Crosley Field	HOUSTON Colt Stad.	HOUSTON Astro-dome	BROOKLYN Ebbets Field	LOS ANGELES L.A. Coliseum	LOS ANGELES Dodger Stad.	MILW.-ATLANTA County Stad.	ATLANTA Atl. Stad.	NEW YORK Polo Grds.	SAN FRAN. Seals Stad.	SAN FRAN. Candle-stk. Pk.
1953	1	0			0			0		0		
1954	11	2			1			0		1		
1955	26	2			2			2		0		
1956	16	3			2 {1 in Ebbets Field / 1 in Roosevelt Stad., J.C.			1		1		
1957	25	2			6			2		1		
1958	30	3				2		1			4	
1959	24	2				6		3			3	
1960	18	1				4		3		NEW YORK METS		3
1961	19	1				1		3				1
1962	19	2	1				1	1		5		1
1963	10	1	0				2	1		0		0
1964	12	1	2				1	4				0
1965	14	2		1			0	3				1
1966	6	2		1			0		3			0
1967	14	0		0			1		0			4
1968	21	1		1			1		2			1
1969	15	2		0			1		1			0
1970	3	0		0			0		0			0
Totals	284	27	3	3	10 / 1 in Roosevelt Stad., J.C. / 11	13	7	24	6	8	7	11

ERNIE BANKS' HOME RUNS BY PARKS (Continued)

YEAR	NEW YORK Shea Stadium	PHILA. Connie Mack St.	PITTS. Forbes Field	Busch Stad.	ST. LOUIS Busch Meml. St.	MONTREAL Jarry Park	SAN DIEGO S.D. Stadium	Total HRs	No. of parks homered in
1953		0	0	1				2	2
1954		1	2	1				19	7
1955		6	0	6				44	6
1956		1	1	3				28	9
1957		3	4	0				43	7
1958		4	2	1				47	8
1959		1	3	3				45	8
1960		7	1	4				41	8
1961		1	1	2				29	8
1962	(see under Polo Grounds)	3	2	2				37	10
1963	0	1	0	3				18	6
1964	1	1	1	1				23	8
1965	1	2	1	3				28	9
1966	1	1	1		0			15	7
1967	1	2	1		0			23	6
1968	0	3	2		0			32	8
1969	1	2	0		0	0	1	23	8
1970	0	0			0	0	0	3	1
Totals	4	39	22	30	0	0	1	500	18

ERNIE BANKS'
HOME RUNS—LIFETIME

	No.	Date	Inn.	On Base	At	Opponent	Pitcher
1953	1	Sept. 20	8	0	A	St. L.	Staley
	2	26	4	0	H	St. L.	Staley
1954	3	Apr. 23	2	0	A	Cin.	Baczewski
	4	May 2²	5	1	H	Pitt.	Friend
	5	12	2	0	A	Phil.	Simmons
	6	16¹	9	1	A	Pitt.	Page
	7	23¹	9	1	H	Mil.	Crone
	8	26	2	0	A	St. L.	Poholsky
	9	31	3	1	H	St. L.	Greason
	10	July 15¹	5	2	H	Pitt.	Surkont
	11	15²	2	0	H	Pitt.	O'Donnell
	12	17¹	8	2	H	Pitt.	Pepper
	13	18	8	0	H	Brk.	Meyer
	14	29	4	2	A	Brk.	Labine
	15	Aug. 1²	6	1	A	Pitt.	Pepper
	16	5	8	0	A	N.Y.	Hearn
	17	12	4	1	A	Cin.	Podbielan
	18	19²	6	0	H	Cin.	Fowler
	19	22	3	0	H	Mil.	Wilson
	20	22	5	0	H	Mil.	Jolly
	21	27	9	0	H	Phil.	Dickson
1955	22	Apr. 14	10	0	A	Cin.	Klippstein
	23	16	2	0	A	St. L.	Poholsky
	24	16	12	0	A	St. L.	Schultz
	25	May 2	2	0	A	Phil.	Roberts
	26	8²	2	0	A	Cin.	Staley
	27	11	1	3	H	Brk.	Meyer
	28	15²	4	0	H	N.Y.	Maglie
	29	18²	4	0	H	Phil.	Dickson
	30	28	6	1	H	Mil.	Nichols
	31	29	3	3	H	Mil.	Burdette

¹ First game of doubleheader.
² Second game of doubleheader.

221

	No.	Date		Inn.	On Base	At	Opponent	Pitcher
	32		30²	7	1	A	St. L.	Jackson
	33	June	1	5	0	A	Phil.	Roberts
	34		2	7	1	A	Phil.	Simmons
	35		12²	7	0	A	Brk.	Labine
	36		21	7	0	A	Brk.	Newcombe
	37		24	3	0	H	Pitt.	Friend
	38		28	1	2	A	Mil.	Spahn
	39		28	3	0	A	Mil.	Spahn
	40	July	1	7	0	H	St. L.	Smith
	41		3²	3	0	H	St. L.	Jones, G.
	42		4¹	9	1	H	Cin.	Fowler
	43		8	1	0	A	St. L.	Woolridge
	44		8	11	1	A	St. L.	Jones, G.
	45		16	1	1	A	Phil.	Roberts
1955	46	July	17¹	6	3	A	Phil.	Negray
	47		17²	4	0	A	Phil.	Simmons
	48		21	9	0	A	Brk.	Bessent
	49		26	3	1	H	N.Y.	Maglie
	50		27²	1	1	H	N.Y.	Monzant
	51		29	8	0	H	Phil.	Meyer
	52		31¹	6	0	H	Phil.	Roberts
	53	Aug.	2	5	3	H	Pitt.	Littlefield
	54		3¹	2	0	H	Pitt.	Face
	55		4	1	1	H	Pitt.	Donoso
	56		4	4	2	H	Pitt.	Surkont
	57		4	8	1	H	Pitt.	Littlefield
	58		5	1	1	H	Brk.	Podres
	59		10²	4	0	H	Cin.	Fowler
	60		11	6	0	H	Cin.	Black
	61	Sept.	2	2	2	H	St. L.	LaPalme
	62		9¹	1	1	H	Brk.	Newcombe
	63		9²	8	0	H	Brk.	Labine
	64		11	4	0	H	N.Y.	Monzant
	65		19	7	3	A	St. L.	McDaniel
1956	66	Apr.	20	2	0	H	Cin.	Fowler
	67		22¹	1	1	H	Cin.	Nuxhall

222

	No.	Date		Inn.	On Base	At	Opponent	Pitcher
	68		29[1]	2	0	A	Cin.	Nuxhall
	69	May	2	5	1	H	N.Y.	Worthington
	70		4	4	1	H	Phil.	Roberts
	71		6[2]	1	1	H	Pitt.	Friend
	72		12	6	1	H	St. L.	Surkont
	73		15	9	1	A	N.Y.	Antonelli
	74		25	7	0	A	St. L.	Dickson
	75		27[1]	5	1	A	St. L.	Poholsky
	76		30[2]	9	0	H	Mil.	Johnson
	77	June	1	7	1	H	Brk.	Labine
	78		8	1	2	H	Phil.	Roberts
	79		9	1	1	H	Phil.	Rogovin
	80		23	7	0	A	Pitt.	Friend
	81		25	1	1	A	Brk.	Erskine
	82		29	1	1	H	Mil.	Burdette
	83		30	6	0	H	Mil.	Conely
	84	July	1[1]	7	0	H	Mil.	Johnson
	85		1[1]	8	1	H	Mil.	Johnson
	86		4[1]	9	0	A	Cin.	Fowler
	87		12[1]	6	0	H	Pitt.	Kline
	88		28	4	0	A	Brk.	Maglie
	89		30[1]	2	0	A	Phil.	Roberts
	90	Aug	6	6	0	A	Mil.	Crone
	91	Sept.	1	4	1	A	Cin.	Lawrence
	92		3[2]	8	0	A	St. L.	Konstanty
	93		29	3	2	H	Cin.	Nuxhall
1957	94	Apr.	24	8	1	A	Cin.	Nuxhall
	95	May	1	6	0	A	Brk.	Drysdale
	96		21	1	1	H	N.Y.	Miller
	97		26[1]	7	1	H	Mil.	Phillips
	98		29	7	0	A	Mil.	Buhl
	99	June	4	8	2	A	Brk.	Koufax
	100		9[1]	8	2	A	Phil.	Roberts
	101		14	8	1	A	Pitt.	Swanson
	102		16[1]	5	0	A	Pitt.	Arroyo
	103		16[2]	4	0	A	Pitt.	Purkey

	No.	Date		Inn.	On Base	At	Opponent	Pitcher
	104		19¹	2	0	H	Phil.	Cardwell
	105		19²	8	0	H	Phil.	Miller
	106		20	6	0	H	Phil.	Haddix
	107		26²	6	1	H	Pitt.	Trimble
	108	July	2	3	0	H	Cin.	Freeman
	109		12	8	1	A	Phil.	Roberts
	110		18	4	0	A	Pitt.	Purkey
	111		19²	4	0	A	Brk.	Maglie
	112		20	7	2	A	Brk.	Drysdale
	113		20	9	0	A	Brk.	Labine
	114		28²	9	0	H	Phil.	Sanford
	115		31²	2	0	H	Brk.	Craig
	116	Aug.	1	4	2	H	Brk.	Koufax
	117		13	8	0	H	St. L.	Schmidt
	118		14	6	0	H	St. L.	Mizell
	119		16	1	2	H	Cin.	Fowler
	120		18	5	1	H	Cin.	Nuxhall
	121		20²	3	1	A	Phil.	Roberts
	122		24	8	0	A	N.Y.	Antonelli
	123		27	1	2	A	Brk.	Newcombe
	124	Sept.	2¹	2	1	H	Mil.	Burdette
	125		2¹	5	0	H	Mil.	Johnson
	126		4¹	5	0	H	Cin.	Podbielan
	127		7	9	0	A	Mil.	Spahn
	128		10	3	0	H	Brk.	Bessent
	129		10	6	2	H	Brk.	Kipp
	130		11	2	0	H	Brk.	Podres
	131		14²	1	0	H	Pitt.	Douglas
	132		14²	4	0	H	Pitt.	Douglas
	133		14²	8	0	H	Pitt.	Purkey
	134		17	3	0	H	Phil.	Sanford
	135		18	4	1	H	Phil.	Roberts
	136		24²	1	1	A	Cin.	Podbielan
1958	137	Apr.	19	6	0	H	St. L.	Mizell
	138		20	3	1	H	St. L.	Wehmeier
	139		22	6	1	A	L.A.	Podres

	No.	Date		Inn.	On Base	At	Opponent	Pitcher
	140		30	3	1	H	Mil.	Buhl
	141		30	7	0	H	Mil.	Jay
	142	May	3	4	0	H	Mil.	Rush
	143		12	3	1	H	St. L.	Barnes
	144		22	2	2	A	Phil.	Sanford
1958	145	May	23	5	1	A	Phil.	Semproch
	146		28	5	0	A	Cin.	Purkey
	147		28	6	1	A	Cin.	Klippstein
	148		30[2]	4	0	H	L.A.	Newcombe
	149		31	5	0	A	L.A.	Erskine
	150	June	3	8	1	H	Phil.	Hearn
	151		4	3	1	H	Phil.	Roberts
	152		4	8	1	H	Phil.	Miller
	153		8	4	0	H	Pitt.	Kline
	154		10	2	2	H	Mil.	Spahn
	155	July	1	1	0	H	S.F.	Antonelli
	156		1	7	0	H	S.F.	Grissom
	157		3	8	0	A	S.F.	Giel
	158		11	7	0	H	Pitt.	Kline
	159		12	2	1	H	Phil.	Semproch
	160		16[2]	1	1	H	Cin.	Lawrence
	161		18	3	2	H	Mil.	Willey
	162		19	2	0	H	Mil.	Jay
	163		25[1]	5	1	A	Mil.	Trowbridge
	164		29	4	1	A	Pitt.	Friend
	165		31	4	0	A	Pitt.	Raydon
	166	Aug.	3[2]	5	2	A	Phil.	Meyer
	167		5	5	0	H	S.F.	Miller
	168		9	1	1	H	St. L.	Maglie
	169		10[1]	3	0	H	St. L.	Muffett
	170		10[2]	3	1	H	St. L.	Jackson
	171		13	6	0	A	L.A.	Koufax
	172		16	5	0	A	S.F.	McCormick
	173		16	8	0	A	S.F.	Jones, G.
	174		17	6	1	A	S.F.	Giel
	175		21	3	2	H	Pitt.	Law

	No.	Date		Inn.	On Base	At	Opponent	Pitcher
	176		21	8	0	H	Pitt.	Blackburn
	177		23	4	0	H	Pitt.	Porterfield
	178		27	6	1	H	Phil.	Simmons
	179	Sept.	3	1	0	H	St. L.	Jackson
	180		7²	7	0	H	S.F.	Gomez
	181		9	5	1	A	St. L.	Jones
	182		13	3	0	A	Cin.	Kellner
	183		17	4	1	A	Phil.	Semproch
1959	184	Apr.	14	4	1	A	S.F.	Sanford
	185		14	8	1	A	S.F.	Sanford
	186		17	7	0	A	L.A.	Williams
	187		18	3	0	A	L.A.	McDevitt
	188		30	10	0	A	Cin.	Lamabe
	189	May	3¹	3	1	A	Phil.	Short
	190		7	6	0	A	St. L.	McDaniel
1959	191	May	13	3	3	H	Cin.	Purkey
	192		17²	5	1	H	Pitt.	Daniels
	193		20	8	2	H	Mil.	Robinson
	194		27	6	0	A	L.A.	Drysdale
	195		28	7	2	A	L.A.	Klippstein
	196	June	5	2	1	A	Pitt.	Blackburn
	197		9	7	1	H	Cin.	Acker
	198		10	9	1	H	Cin.	Pena
	199		12	1	0	H	Mil.	Burdette
	200		14	7	1	H	Mil.	Willey
	201		16	4	0	H	Pitt.	Friend
	202		19	6	1	H	Phil.	Conley
	203		25	6	0	A	Cin.	Purkey
	204		27	7	0	A	Mil.	Jay
	205	July	2	6	2	H	S.F.	Jones, G.
	206		5²	4	0	H	L.A.	Williams
	207		11	4	0	A	Pitt.	Kline
	208		16	4	0	H	Mil.	Burdette
	209		21	9	0	A	St. L.	Blaylock
	210		26	3	1	A	S.F.	McCormick
	211		29	4	0	A	Mil.	Burdette

	No.	Date	Inn.	On Base	At	Opponent	Pitcher
	212	29	6	2	A	Mil.	Burdette
	213	Aug. 5	6	0	H	Phil.	Conley
	214	7	3	0	H	Pitt.	Kline
	215	9	2	0	H	Pitt.	Law
	216	11	5	1	H	L.A.	Podres
	217	12	1	2	H	L.A.	Drysdale
	218	14	7	1	H	S.F.	Byerly
	219	16	1	1	H	S.F.	Antonelli
	220	17	1	1	A	Pitt.	Haddix
	221	29	3	3	H	Mil.	Spahn
	222	Sept. 6[1]	10	2	A	L.A.	Koufax
	223	6[2]	8	0	A	L.A.	Sherry
	224	13	3	0	H	St. L.	Hughes
	225	17	6	0	H	Phil.	Roberts
	226	21	4	0	A	St. L.	Broglio
	227	23	1	1	H	S.F.	Antonelli
	228	25	8	0	H	L.A.	McDevitt
1960	229	Apr. 13	4	0	A	L.A.	Sherry
	230	14	3	3	A	S.F.	Sanford
	231	19	3	0	A	St. L.	Mizell
	232	29	7	2	A	St. L.	Miller
	233	29	9	2	A	St. L.	Barnes
	234	May 13	6	0	H	St. L.	Kline
	235	15[2]	6	1	H	St. L.	McDaniel
	236	17	1	2	A	Pitt.	Friend
	237	21	3	0	A	Mil.	Jay
	238	31	1	0	A	S.F.	Antonelli
1960	239	June 2	5	0	A	L.A.	Drysdale
	240	3	8	0	A	L.A.	Rakow
	241	4	3	1	A	L.A.	Williams
	242	9	6	1	H	Pitt.	Friend
	243	10	3	1	H	Phil.	Owens
	244	11	7	0	H	Phil.	Short
	245	14	4	0	A	Mil.	Buhl
	246	19[2]	3	1	A	Cin.	McLish
	247	21[1]	3	1	A	Phil.	Owens

ERNIE BANKS' H.R.—Lifetime (Continued)

	No.	Date		Inn.	On Base	At	Opponent	Pitcher
	248		21[1]	7	0	A	Phil.	Owens
	249		23	6	0	A	Phil.	Green
	250		30	6	1	H	Mil.	McMahon
	251	July	2	7	1	H	Cin.	Purkey
	252		5	6	1	H	St. L.	McDaniel
	253		6	2	2	H	St. L.	Gibson
	254		9	12	0	A	S.F.	Antonelli
	255		22	5	1	H	Mil.	Burdette
	256		26	7	0	H	Phil.	Roberts
	257	Aug.	3[2]	1	1	H	Cin.	Hook
	258		4	6	1	H	Cin.	McLish
	259		12	3	0	A	Phil.	Roberts
	260		13	8	0	A	Phil.	Mahaffey
	261		14[2]	1	1	A	Phil.	Green
	262		17	9	0	H	L.A.	Drysdale
	263		21[2]	4	1	H	S.F.	Maranda
	264		25	2	0	H	Pitt.	Mizell
	265		30	9	0	H	Cin.	Nuxhall
	266	Sept.	2	3	0	A	St. L.	Jackson
	267		8	4	0	A	Phil.	Mahaffey
	268		15	5	0	A	Mil.	Burdette
	269		17	4	1	H	L.A.	Koufax
1961	270	Apr.	19	7	0	A	Pitt.	Friend
	271		22	6	0	A	Phil.	Short
	272		29	9	0	A	L.A.	Podres
	273	May	3	5	0	H	S.F.	O'Dell
	274		3	7	0	H	S.F.	Bolin
	275		9	1	2	A	Mil.	Buhl
	276		9	6	0	A	Mil.	Buhl
	277		28	8	3	H	S.F.	Miller, S.
	278	June	4[2]	1	0	A	Cin.	O'Toole
	279		5	8	0	A	St. L.	McDaniel
	280		7	9	1	A	St. L.	Cicotte
	281		17	6	0	A	S.F.	O'Dell
	282	July	7	2	1	H	Phil.	Short
	283		26	8	2	H	St. L.	Bauta

	No.	Date	Inn.	On Base	At	Opponent	Pitcher
	284	28	4	0	H	Cin.	O'Toole
	285	28	6	0	H	Cin.	O'Toole
	286	29	3	0	H	Cin.	Jay
1961	287	Aug. 2²	1	1	H	Mil.	Buhl
	288	3	9	1	H	Mil.	Burdette
	289	14	2	1	H	Phil.	Sullivan
	290	15	1	1	H	Phil.	Mahaffey
	291	17¹	1	0	H	Pitt.	Mizell
	292	17¹	3	1	H	Pitt.	Mizell
	293	Sept. 2	7	0	H	S.F.	Sanford
	294	3	4	1	H	Mil.	Burdette
	295	4	3	1	H	Mil.	Willey
	296	7	4	0	H	Pitt.	Haddix
	297	19	9	1	A	L.A.	Drysdale
	298	24²	6	0	A	Mil.	Hendley
1962	299	Apr. 10	7	0	A	Hou.	Shantz
	300	18	10	0	H	Hou.	Farrell
	301	22¹	1	2	A	St. L.	Sadecki
	302	25	8	0	H	L.A.	Sherry
	303	26	1	1	H	L.A.	Richert
	304	May 5	8	1	H	S.F.	Duffalo
	305	13²	1	0	H	Phil.	Short
	306	15	6	0	A	N.Y.	Mizell
	307	16	3	1	A	N.Y.	Hillman
	308	18	3	0	A	Phil.	Bennett
	309	20²	5	2	A	Phil.	Hamilton
	310	29	3	1	H	Mil.	Hendley
	311	29	5	0	H	Mil.	Nottebart
	312	29	7	0	H	Mil.	Burdette
	313	June 10²	9	2	H	N.Y.	Anderson
	314	15	6	0	A	N.Y.	Craig
	315	16	4	0	A	N.Y.	Hunter
	316	17¹	3	0	A	N.Y.	Jackson
	317	22	6	0	A	Pitt.	Gibbon
	318	24²	5	0	A	Pitt.	Lamabe
	319	25	3	2	H	St. L.	Washburn

	No.	Date	Inn.	On Base	At	Opponent	Pitcher
	320	July 2[1]	4	1	H	Cin.	Purkey
	321	17	7	0	A	St. L.	McDaniel
	322	22	3	2	H	L.A.	Moeller
	323	25	2	1	H	Phil.	Bennett
	324	25	4	0	H	Phil.	Bennett
	325	Aug. 5[1]	4	0	A	L.A.	Ortega
	326	8	1	1	A	Mil.	Hendley
	327	11	6	0	H	Pitt.	Law
	328	14	2	0	H	S.F.	Sanford
	329	15	5	2	H	S.F.	O'Dell
	330	Sept. 5[1]	6	0	A	Cin.	Maloney
	331	9	2	0	A	S.F.	McCormick
	332	14	3	2	H	L.A.	Podres
	333	17	7	2	H	St. L.	Washburn
	334	20[2]	5	1	A	Phil.	Hamilton
	335	29	2	0	H	N.Y.	Miller, R. L.
1963	336	Apr. 16	5	0	A	L.A.	Podres
	337	28	8	0	H	Phil.	Short
	338	May 1	1	2	A	St. L.	Sadecki
	339	1	7	2	A	St. L.	Fanok
	340	3	9	0	A	Mil.	Raymond
	341	7	2	0	H	Pitt.	Cardwell
	342	18	8	1	H	Mil.	Hendley
	343	25	6	0	H	Hou.	Farrell
	344	June 5[1]	4	1	H	S.F.	Fisher
	345	5[1]	7	0	H	S.F.	Perry
	346	9	2	0	H	L.A.	Koufax
	347	9	5	0	H	L.A.	Koufax
	348	9	9	1	H	L.A.	Sherry
	349	14	6	0	A	L.A.	Miller
	350	19	1	1	H	Hou.	Brown, H.
	351	July 12	6	0	A	Cin.	O'Toole
	352	14[2]	8	1	A	St. L.	Schultz
	353	Aug. 14[1]	2	1	A	Phil.	Culp
1964	354	Apr. 15	7	2	A	Pitt.	Sisk
	355	19	4	0	H	Phil.	Bennett, D.

	No.	Date	Inn.	On Base	At	Opponent	Pitcher
	356	May 10[1]	4	0	H	Hou.	Nottebart
	357	24[1]	4	0	A	Cin.	O'Toole
	358	30[1]	7	0	H	Mil.	Sadowski
	359	June 6	7	2	A	Mil.	Spahn
	360	7	4	1	A	Mil.	Lemaster
	361	24	5	0	A	Phil.	Bennett, D.
	362	26	4	2	H	Hou.	Johnson, K.
	363	28[1]	5	1	H	Hou.	Brown
	364	July 14	2	0	H	N.Y.	Jackson
	365	19[1]	2	1	A	L.A.	Ortega
	366	26	4	1	A	Hou.	Johnson, K.
	367	Aug. 11	5	2	H	Phil.	Culp
	368	13	2	0	H	Phil.	Bennett
	369	26	4	0	A	Hou.	Brown
	370	28	3	1	H	N.Y.	Fisher
	371	29	6	0	H	N.Y.	Cisco
	372	Sept. 5	2	0	A	St. L.	Cuellar
	373	12	6	1	H	St. L.	Craig
	374	19[1]	4	0	A	Mil.	Fischer
	375	20	4	0	A	Mil.	Blasingame
	376	27[2]	5	3	H	S.F.	Bolin
1965	377	Apr. 12	9	2	H	St. L.	Schultz
	378	15	5	0	A	Mil.	Sadowski
	379	19	5	1	A	St. L.	Taylor
	380	May 1[1]	5	1	A	Hou.	Johnson, K.
	381	7	1	2	H	Hou.	Giusti
	382	8	2	0	H	Hou.	Nottebart
	383	9[2]	4	0	H	Hou.	Bruce
	384	9[2]	6	0	H	Hou.	Bruce
	385	25	2	0	A	Pitt.	Friend
	386	30	2	0	A	Phil.	Herbert
	387	June 9	6	2	H	Mil.	Blasingame
	388	19	5	0	A	Cin.	Maloney
	389	20[2]	8	1	A	Cin.	McCool
	390	July 11[2]	1	2	H	St. L.	Sadecki
	391	22	2	0	H	Phil.	Herbert

	No.	Date		Inn.	On Base	At	Opponent	Pitcher
	392		27	5	0	H	N.Y.	Kroll
	393		28¹	1	1	H	N.Y.	Parsons
	394	Aug.	8¹	6	1	A	N.Y.	Fisher
	395		15	2	0	H	Mil.	Johnson
	396		25	7	0	A	St. L.	Gibson
	397		26	6	0	A	St. L.	Purkey
	398		29	6	0	A	Mil.	Fischer
	399		29	8	2	A	Mil.	Osinski
	400	Sept.	2	3	2	H	St. L.	Simmons
	401		12¹	4	0	A	S.F.	Bolin
	402		21	1	0	H	Phil.	Jackson
	403		23²	9	1	H	Phil.	Short
	404		29	8	0	A	Phil.	Culp
1966	405	May	20	2	0	A	Atl.	Lemaster
	406		20	9	0	A	Atl.	Lemaster
	407	June	21	4	1	H	S.F.	Marichal
	408		22²	8	1	H	S.F.	Herbel
	409	July	28	9	1	A	Cin.	Nottebart
	410		30	9	0	A	N.Y.	Ribant
	411	Aug.	4	1	2	H	Atl.	Lemaster
	412		6	8	0	H	S.F.	McDaniel
	413		17	10	2	A	Phil.	Buhl
	414		19	4	0	H	Pitt.	Law
	415		27	8	1	A	Hou.	Raymond
	416		30	3	2	A	Atl.	Jay
	417	Sept.	1	4	0	A	Cin.	Pappas
	418		4	1	2	A	Pitt.	Fryman
	419		18	4	1	H	St. L.	Jaster
1967	420	Apr.	12	6	0	H	Phil.	Jackson, L.
	421		14	2	0	A	Pitt.	Ribant
	422	May	7	4	0	H	St. L.	Gibson
	423		8	2	0	H	S.F.	Marichal
	424		12	2	0	A	L.A.	Osteen
	425		15	9	2	A	S.F.	Linzy
	426		21¹	2	0	H	L.A.	Brewer
	427	June	5	9	0	A	Phil.	Jackson, G.

	No.	Date	Inn.	On Base	At	Opponent	Pitcher
	428	11^2	6	2	H	N.Y.	Estrada
	429	14	7	0	H	L.A.	Osteen
	430	18^1	3	1	A	N.Y.	Shaw, R.
	431	23	7	0	H	Hou.	Latman
	432	25^2	6	1	H	Hou.	Belinsky
	433	25^2	7	1	H	Hou.	Eilers
	434	29	6	1	H	Pitt.	Mikkelsen
	435	July 16^1	1	2	A	S.F.	Perry
	436	16^2	2	1	A	S.F.	Herbel
	437	23^2	5	1	H	S.F.	Herbel
	438	Aug. 2^1	9	0	H	St. L.	Hughes
	439	20	4	2	A	Phil.	Hall
	440	Sept. 4^1	11	0	H	L.A.	Sutton
	441	9	5	1	A	S.F.	McCormick
	442	23	5	1	H	Cin.	Tsitouris
1968	443	Apr. 14	1	2	H	St. L.	Hughes
	444	16	5	0	H	Cin.	Lee
	445	29	7	0	A	Pitt.	Blass
	446	May 2	6	0	A	Pitt.	Bunning
	447	13	6	1	A	L.A.	Singer
	448	19^2	6	2	A	S.F.	Gibbon
	449	26	1	1	H	S.F.	McCormick
	450	26	4	0	H	S.F.	McCormick
	451	June 5	6	0	H	N.Y.	Seaver
	452	10	2	0	H	Cin.	Nolan
	453	10	4	0	H	Cin.	Nolan
	454	13	3	1	H	Cin.	Cloninger
	455	July 7^1	1	3	H	Pitt.	Blass
	456	17^1	1	2	A	Phil.	Fryman
	457	17^1	5	1	A	Phil.	Farrell
	458	30	3	1	H	S.F.	Sadecki
	459	31	4	0	H	Hou.	Lemaster
	460	31	6	0	H	Hou.	Ray
	461	Aug. 5	6	0	A	Atl.	Pappas
	462	7	9	0	A	Atl.	Stone
	463	11	6	0	A	Cin.	Maloney

	No.	Date	Inn.	On Base	At	Opponent	Pitcher
	464	16	8	1	H	Cin.	Carroll
	465	19	1	1	H	Atl.	Stone
	466	21¹	2	0	H	Atl.	Pappas
	467	21¹	7	1	H	Atl.	Upshaw
	468	24	5	0	A	Hou.	Giusti
	469	Sept. 3	7	1	H	S.F.	Monbouquette
	470	4²	1	2	H	S.F.	Herbel
	471	6	6	0	H	Phil.	Wise
	472	8	5	0	H	Phil.	James
	473	10	7	0	H	N.Y.	Ryan
	474	13²	3	1	A	Phil.	Johnson, J.
1969	475	Apr. 8	1	2	H	Phil.	Short
	476	8	3	1	H	Phil.	Short
	477	May 13	1	2	H	S.D.	Kelley
	478	13	5	2	H	S.D.	Everitt
	479	14	9	0	H	S.D.	Podres
	480	20	9	1	A	L.A.	Purdin
	481	24	5	3	A	S.D.	Baldschun
	482	June 4	2	0	H	Hou.	Griffin
	483	6	1	2	H	Cin.	Cloninger
	484	7	1	1	H	Cin.	Merritt
	485	13	3	0	A	Cin.	Culver
	486	14	5	1	A	Cin.	Cloninger
	487	29²	1	2	H	St. L.	Grant
	488	July 8	6	0	A	N.Y.	Koosman
	489	18	1	2	A	Phil.	Fryman
	490	31	4	1	H	S.F.	Bolin
	491	Aug. 23	4	0	H	Hou.	Griffin
	492	24¹	2	0	H	Hou.	Billingham
	493	24¹	8	1	H	Hou.	Gladding
	494	26	4	0	H	Cin.	Merritt
	495	30	1	1	A	Atl.	Reed
	496	Sept. 11	8	0	A	Phil.	James
	497	Oct. 2	6	2	H	N.Y.	Cardwell
1970	498	Apr. 25	3	2	H	Hou.	Bouton
	499	May 9	7	1	H	Cin.	Gullett

234

No.	Date		Inn.	On Base	At	Opponent	Pitcher
500		12	2	0	H	Atl.	Jarvis
501		30[2]	4	0	H	S.D.	Dobson
502	June	13	2	0	A	L.A.	Osteen
503		14	2	0	A	L.A.	Singer
504		17	8	2	A	S.F.	Davison
505		24[1]	9	2	H	N.Y.	Seaver
506		29	6	1	A	St. L.	Carlton
507		29	8	1	A	St. L.	Carlton
508	Sept.	5	9	1	H	N.Y.	Koosman
509		10	4	2	H	Mont.	O'Donoghue

235

Credits